Corner House Publishers

SOCIAL SCIENCE REPRINTS

General Editor MAURICE FILLER

To
THE MEMORY
OF
MARK TWAIN

Hail, rosy laughter! thou deserv'st the bays!
Come, with thy dimples, animate these lays,
While universal peals attest thy praise.
Daughter of Joy! thro' thee we health attain,
When Esculapian recipes are vain.

Jonathan Mitchell Sewall (1748-1808)

of New Hampshire

THE WIT
AND HUMOR
OF
COLONIAL DAYS

CARL HOLLIDAY

CORNER HOUSE PUBLISHERS

WILLIAMSTOWN, MASSACHUSETTS 01267

1975

FIRST PUBLISHED IN 1912

REPRINTED 1975

BY

CORNER HOUSE PUBLISHERS

ISBN 0-87928-058-1

Printed in the United States of America

PREFACE

If there is any branch of literature in which America has excelled other modern nations, it is humor. It is doubtful, for instance, whether any other nation has produced during the last half-century a wit surpassing Josh Billings in shrewd sarcasm, Artemus Ward in ridiculous extravagance, or Mark Twain in solemn statement of the outrageously untrue. This ability in the American, however, of " seeing the point " is by no means a development of the last half-century. It is as old as the nation. The colonists had scarcely landed in Virginia before witty letters telling of ludicrous sights and mishaps in the raw settlement began to go back to England; while in New England there soon was heard a taunting satire like that of the Hebrew prophets of old. Nor has the stream of wit and humor once ceased from that day to this. Faithfully, too, this type of literature has served the nation in every crisis. It has ridiculed our foes, encouraged our defend-

5

ers, and turned the hardships of war into causes of merriment. In great political struggles it has laughed hypocrisy, bombast, and dangerous movements out of court. In times of peace it has proved its value in maintaining decent standards, in driving silly and foppish tendencies from our midst, and in showing us ourselves as we really are.

In spite of this, however, and in spite, also, of the variety and richness of the humor which we have added to the world's literature, there has been scarcely a line written concerning its development in this nation. Other peoples, notably the French and the English, possess such studies of their fun-makers; but here in America, where everybody is something of a humorist, students of literature seem to have looked upon the subject as one beneath the dignity of serious investigation. Surely the element which has entered into the very woof of our literature and which has become a distinguishing characteristic of us as a nation is worthy of no small attention.

In the present work I trace the course of our wit and humor from the days of the first settlement up to the opening of the nineteenth century. At some future time I hope to continue the story through two other periods, dealing in the one with the Early National Humor up to the Civil War, and in the other with Modern American Humor. In the volume now presented I believe I show that the current idea of colonial sombreness is, happily, very incorrect; that our forefathers of Revolutionary days enjoyed a laugh and often indulged; and that their wit and humor did a work in the founding and maintaining of the Republic not yet recognized even in the more detailed histories on this period.

In several instances I am indebted to Duyckinck's *Cyclopædia of American Literature* and to those admirable works by Moses Coit Tyler, *A History of American Literature during the Colonial Times,* and *The Literary History of the American Revolution.* Without these books I could hardly have secured some of the biographical details contained in this volume. My thanks for assistance most kindly rendered are due Miss Mary Hannah Johnson, Librarian of the Nashville Carnegie Library, and Dr. Richard Jones, recently of Vanderbilt University.

PREFACE

Now, in conclusion, if you, the " gentle reader," fail to see the humor of the old times, as discussed in this book, I pray you remember the words of Shakespeare, that

> " A jest's prosperity *lies in the ear*
> *Of him that hears it,* never in the tongue
> Of him that makes it."

CARL HOLLIDAY

VANDERBILT UNIVERSITY
NASHVILLE, TENNESSEE

CONTENTS

EARLY COLONIAL HUMOR

CONTENTS

CONTENTS

11

CONTENTS

CONTENTS

CONTENTS

The Wit and Humor of Colonial Days

EARLY COLONIAL HUMOR

I

The usual way to begin a book dealing with humor is, I believe, to make a painstaking discrimination between wit and humor. This, however, I decline to do, for two reasons: First, because I have never been able to find or make a very good definition of either; and, second, because any reader who has not the ability to know either one when he sees it doubtless would not possess acumen enough to understand any such discussion as I might undertake. This book is not intended for his kind, anyway.

I intend simply to tell of the development of humor among our forefathers from their coming in 1607 to the days when their children had the Republic in pretty fair working order, say,

about 1800; in short, as a ballad of the times
puts it,

> " When these free states were colonies
> Unto the mother nation;
> And in Connecticut the good
> Old Blue Laws were in fashion."

And, now, not to waste time on preliminaries,
let us hasten back to those "Pilgrim Father"
days, choose a sarcastic Puritan, and smile with
him, or at him.

Who cracked the first joke in America? The
early records do not state. We are not even
quite sure as to the first American who tried to
be funny on paper. Of course, some of the
very earliest colonists in both Virginia and
New England wrote humorous and sarcastic
accounts back home, and the ludicrous situations portrayed in these are not lost upon us
of a later date. One might call to mind John
Pory of the Jamestown settlement, whose letters to the " home folks " were quaintly
witty; Francis Higginson, sturdy old New
Englander, in his " True Relation " (1629),
and his " New England Plantations " (1629),
sometimes came dangerously near joking; and

some students of American literature would say that William Wood of Massachusetts, by his sprightly "New England's Prospect" (1634), deserves the place as first of the numerous " fathers of American humor." But the first man to do it with malice aforethought and with the intention of publishing also, seems to have been the New England preacher Nathaniel Ward (1578-1652).

NATHANIEL WARD

The first of our American satirists was no mere laughing fool. Few men of those grave and stubborn colonial days had received a better mental training for civil and theological strife, and few had held themselves more persistently to an uncomfortably stormy career. Your true Puritan fought sin and everything else in the neighborhood, and Nathaniel Ward was not an exception. He graduated at Emmanuel College, Cambridge, and old Bishop Fuller has spoken of him as one of the most learned writers in the ancient institution. But his was a knowledge far wider than the range of books. He had travelled the nations of Europe and had conversed with their leaders; he had attended the lectures of that daring theologian, Paræus of Heidelberg; he was a good friend of Francis Bacon's; and he had been so intimate with royalty that he had held in his arms the infant Prince Rupert, the swaggering cavalier of Cromwell's day.

For some years Ward had been a lawyer, and if the trend of the times had not been toward religious discussions, his subtle reasoning power might have made him one of the greatest jurists of the century. But the question "What think ye of Christ?" was on every man's lips, and Ward felt called upon, like many another brilliant intellect of that stern era, to explain the Higher Law. For ten years he fervently "wagged his pow in a pulpit"— ten stormy years harassed by the watchful eye of that terror of lax Churchmen, Archbishop Laud, who sent innumerable bits of advice and innumerable warnings to the little rectory at Stondon Massey in Essex; for the future pioneer of American satire was a trifle too original in his theological views to suit the theologically sensitive old bishop, and the tenor of their way was not always that of brotherly love.

At length the crisis came. In 1633 the Archbishop summoned the rector, bitterly rebuked him for having anti-Christ theories, silenced him (technically but not actually), and excommunicated him for non-conformity. Naturally Ward looked to the hills of Masachusetts, whence came his help; everybody who dissented in those days did that. And so it happened that early in 1634 Nathaniel Ward, preacher, satirist, and " pig-headed " citizen, took charge of the little church at Aggawam (now Ipswich), Massachusetts, and began to impress upon the people of the commonwealth the fact that something in the nature of a human firebrand had fallen in their midst. His friends called it godly zeal; but his enemies designated it plain pig-headedness. Perhaps it was both.

We may not enter into a detailed account of his varied activities; he seemed to have a hand in everything. History tells us, for one thing, that he helped John Cotton and other Puritan leaders draw up that strange code of laws with the misleading title of " Body of Liberties." This decidedly unhumorous deed was done in 1641, but five years later he wrote, doubtless as a recompense, the first American book of

humor, the *Simple Cobbler of Aggawam,* a
work showing how badly, according to the cobbler's views, the world was theologically and
socially out of joint. Other books he composed, but as they deal extensively in promises
of volcanic landscapes in the next world, they
cannot with propriety be called funny. Ward
returned to England in 1647, and there, in 1652,
was gathered to his fathers, several of whom
were preachers, and who therefore doubtless
missed entirely the scenery just mentioned, or
else caught but distant glimpses of it from the
windows of the Heaven-bound observation car.

This *Simple Cobbler* is a most sarcastic fellow. It turns out that he had been " a solitary widower almost twelve years," and perhaps that explains some of his bitter jokes. He
is especially biting when discussing the fashions affected by ladies of the early seventeenth
century:

" Should I not keep promise in speaking a
little to women's fashions, they would take it
unkindly. I was loath to pester better matter
with such stuff; I rather thought it meet to let
them stand by themselves, like the *Quae genus*
in the grammar, being deficients or redundants,

not to be brought under any rule: I shall therefore make bold for this once, to borrow a little of their loose-tongued Liberty, and misspend a word or two upon their long-waisted, but short-skirted Patience. . . .

> Gray Gravity itself can well beteem
> That Language be adapted to the theme.
> He that to Parrots speakes, must parrotise;
> He that instructs a Fool, may act th' unwise.

" It is known more than enough that I am neither Niggard, nor Cynic, to the due bravery of the true gentry. I honor the woman that can honor herself with her attire; a good text always deserves a fair margin; I am not much offended if I see a trim fur trimmer than she that wears it. In a word, whatever Christianity or Civility will allow, I can afford with London measure; but when I hear a nugiperous gentledame inquire what dress the Queen is in this week: what the nudiustertian fashion of the Court; with egg [desire] to be in it in all haste, whatever it be; I look at her as the very gizzard of a trifle, the product of a quarter of a cipher, the epitome of Nothing, fitter to be kicked, if she were a kickable substance, than either honored or humored.''

21

It is evident that, besides being a widower, friend Ward must have been a dyspeptic. The world is out of joint, and woman has had a large share in this anatomical catastrophe. There are in her certain traits that the sarcastic Puritan cannot at all comprehend.

"To speak moderately," says he, "I truly confess it is beyond the ken of my understanding to conceive how those women should have any true grace or valuable virtue, that have so little wit, as to disfigure themselves with such exotic garb, as not only dismantles their native lovely lustre, but transclouts them into gant-bar-geese, ill-shapen, shotten shell-fish, Egyptian hieroglyphics, or at the best into French flurts of the pastery, which a proper English woman should scorn with her heels. It is no marvel they wear drailes on the hinder part of their heads, having nothing as it seems in the fore part but a few squirrels' brains to help them frisk from one ill-favored fashion to another. . . . I can make myself sick at any time with comparing the dazzling splendor wherewith our gentle-women were embellished in some former habits, with the gut-foundered goose-dom wherewith they are now surcingled and

debauched.   We have about five or six of them
in our Colony; if I see any of them accidentally,
I cannot cleanse my fancy of them for a month
after. . . . Methinks it should break the hearts
of Englishmen to see so many goodly English
women imprisoned in French cages peering out
of their hood-holes for some men of mercy to
help them with a little wit, and nobody relieves
them.''

Now and again Ward's emotions become too
fervid for prose: he bursts into *poetry:*

'' The world is full of care, much like unto a bubble,
    Women and care, and care and Women,
And Women and care and trouble.''

Thus the '' cobbler '' proceeds, pegging the
foibles of his day and oftentimes speaking with
a Franklin-like bluntness and common-sense.
In fact, there is considerable resemblance between Ward's ideas and expressions and those
of Poor Richard.   While paying his respects to
the ladies and their fashions he does not forget
the tailors.   He fears for these knights of the
needle:

'' It is a more common than convenient saying that nine tailors make a man; it were well

23

if nineteen could make a woman to her mind.
If tailors were men indeed, well furnished but
with mere moral principles, they would disdain
to be led about like Apes, by such mimic Mar-
mosets. It is a most unworthy thing for men
that have bones in them, to spend their lives in
making fiddle cases for futilous women's
fancies; which are the very pettitoes of in-
firmity, the giblets of perquisquilian toys. . . .
It is no little labor to be continually putting up
English women into outlandish casks; who if
they be not shifted anew once in a few months,
grow too sour for their husbands. What this
trade will answer for themselves when God
shall take measure of tailors' consciences is
beyond my skill to imagine. . . . He that makes
coats for the moon, had need take measure
every noon; and he that makes for women, as
often, to keep them from lunacy.''

I quote thus freely from Ward's opinion on
women, not to arouse the ire of the female
perambulating fashion plates of to-day, but
simply to show that the stern Pilgrim fathers
did, after all, have some sort of humor, even
if a grim sort. Our histories so often leave
the impression that the Puritan was merely a

funereal creature, the deadly enemy of mince-pie and plum-pudding, that it is well to refer to the ancient writings now and then and see for ourselves that they dared to smile, and that right often.

Many were the faults and human weaknesses attacked by this first of American satirists. Indeed, he seemed to look upon himself as divinely appointed scolder plenipotentiary to the world at large. Hear a few complimentary remarks concerning the Hibernians:

" These Irish, anciently called Anthropophagi (man-eaters), have a tradition among them, that when the Devil showed our Saviour all the Kingdoms of the Earth and their glory, he would not show him Ireland, but reserved it for himself; it is probably true, for he hath kept it ever since for his own peculiar; the old Fox foresaw it would eclipse the glory of all the rest. . . . They are the very offal of men, dregs of mankind, reproach of Christendom, the bots that crawl on the beasts' tail."

We must not think that Nathaniel Ward was a satirist and nothing else. Often he turned from his scoffing and sarcasm to call down the curse of God upon England's enemies and to

speak with heartfelt earnestness of the folly
and sin about him. Satire and humor have
ever been a mighty weapon in the political,
social and general reform movements of America, and this first American book of wit is no
exception. Running through four editions
within the first year of its existence and arousing the men of two lands to a determined frame
of mind, its value in its own day cannot be
doubted, and even yet, as Tyler declares in his
History of American Literature, " it is a tremendous partisan pamphlet, intensely vital,
. . . full of fire, wit, whim, eloquence, sarcasm,
invective, patriotism, bigotry." The scolding,
rabid " Simple Cobbler " was violently in
earnest; the day of judgment was at hand.
Hear his first sentence: " Either I am in an
apoplexy or that man is in a lethargy, who doth
not now sensibly feel God shaking the heavens
over his head and the earth under his feet."
He saw political ruin threatening England, in-
sanity hovering over every woman, and heresy
stalking into every church. Beware, cried he,
beware of false prophets! " He usually hears
best in their meetings, that stops his ears
closest; he opens his mouth to the best purpose

that keeps it shut; and he doeth best of all that declines their company as wisely as he may. . . . Here I hold myself bound to set up a beacon to give warning of a new-sprung sect of phrantastics, which would persuade themselves and others that they have discovered the Nor-West passage to Heaven?''

Certainly our first satirist was a worshipper of sincerity. His heart was in his book, and he spoke straight from that heart; his words need no interpreter. Of course, his learning got the better of him at times, but that was a common fault among the prose writers of the seventeenth century. For instance, years ago Professor Moses Coit Tyler defied any man to explain this expression of Ward's: '' If the whole conclave of hell can so compromise ex-adverse and diametrical contradictions as to compolitize such a multimonstrous maufrey of heteroclites and quicquidlibets quietly, I trust I may say with all humble reverence, they can do more than the senate of heaven.'' How old Dr. Johnson would have enjoyed that sentence! But we have seen that this was not Ward's usual manner of procedure; for his soul was too heated for such verbal jugglery.

27

Thus this early American wit lashed the fallen sons of Adam. Wrong he often was; narrow we must consider him in this day; blindly obstinate his enemies thought him in his own time. But beneath all his mistakes and natural failings we may frequently perceive that same plain, homely and earthy philosophy, that assumed yet shrewd simplicity, which have made us smile with Franklin and Josh Billings and Artemus Ward and many another American wiseacre. It has been a valuable and brilliantly original brood that grumbling old Nathaniel Ward fathered.

THOMAS MORTON

Right in the beginning the reader must understand that many a fledgling wit of these first days must go unnoticed; else we should have a work as large as a family Bible and, perhaps, just as grave and solemn. One is tempted, for instance, to linger over the literary efforts of Thomas Morton (1634), who scandalized all New England by raising a May-pole eighty feet high at Merry Mount, brewing " a barrel of excellent beer," and shouting with his companions such Bacchanalian verses as

" Drink and be merry, merry, merry, boys,
Let all your delight be in Hymen's joys,
Io to Hymen now the day is come,
About the Merry May-pole take a roame

. . . .

Nectar is a thing assign'd,
By the Deities own mind,
To cure the heart opprest with grief,
And of good liquors is the chief
Then drink, etc.
Io to Hymen, etc."

29

We may not stay to wonder over the many statements in his quaint volume *New English Canaan;* such as his interesting discovery that the beaver must sit " in his house built on the water with his tayle hanging in the water, which else would over-heate and rot off."

Then, too, we should find much cause for astonishment in the epitaphs of those grave days. When Reverend Mr. Samuel Stone of Hartford died, a friend thus sang his praise:

" A stone more than the Ebenezer fam'd;
 Stone splendent diamond, right orient named;
 A cordial stone, that often cheered hearts
 With pleasant wit, with Gospel rich imparts;
 Whetstone, that edgify'd th' obtusest mind;
 Loadstone that drew the iron heart unkind;
 A pond'rous stone, that would the bottom sound
 Of Scripture depths, and bring out Arcan's found;
 A stone for kingly David's use so fit,
 As would not fail Goliah's front to hit."

And again, when John Sherman of New Haven, preacher, mathematician, almanac-maker, and father of twenty-six children, heard of the death of his good friend Mitchell, a Harvard pastor, he exclaimed (after due thought and many poetic pangs):

" Here lies the darling of his time,
Mitchell expired in his prime;
Who four years short of forty-seven,
Was found full ripe and pluck'd for heaven."

When Thomas Dudley, father of our first poetess, Anne Bradstreet, came to his death-bed, he showed where his daughter had received her surprising gift, by composing such farewell lines as

" Dim eyes, deaf ears, cold stomach shew
My dissolution is in view;
Eleven times seven near lived have I,
And now God calls, I willing die."

Nor may we stop to laugh with William Wood over the quaint wit in his *New England's Prospect* (1634), wherein he speaks with rare discernment concerning

" The kingly Lion, and the strong-armed Bear,
The large-limbed Mooses, with the tripping Deer;
Quill-darting Porcupines and Raccoons be
Castled in the hollow of an aged tree;

. . . .

The grim-face Ounce, and ravenous, howling Wolf
Whose meagre paunch sucks like a swallowing
  gulf."

31

He has much, also, to say about the red man: —very amusing, too, save to an Indian. " A sagamore with a hum-bird in his ear for a pendant, a black-hawk on his occiput for his plume, mowhackees for his gold chain, good store of wampompeage begirting his loins, his bow in his hand, his quiver at his back, with six naked Indian spatter-lashes at his heels for his guard, thinks himself little inferior to the great Cham; he will not stick to say he is all one with King Charles. He thinks he can blow down castles with his breath, and conquer kingdoms with his conceit."

Those were strange old days around Boston town. As has been said by plain, blunt Benjamin Thompson of Harvard, another of the colonial wits whom we must neglect,

" 'Twas in those days an honest grace would hold
   Till an hot pudding grew at heart a-cold.
   And men had better stomachs at religion,
   Than I to capon, turkey-cock, or pigeon;
   When honest sisters met to pray, not prate,
   About their own and not their neighbor's state."

Doubtless many who would have liked to laugh remained to pray, and learned from these pudding spoilers and superhuman women to fear all signs of levity.

The habitual humorist was, however, not such an *avis rara* in early colonial days as our histories would teach. The first efforts of the Virginia colony were so full of disaster and sorrow, and the founders of the New England provinces were so impressed with the seriousness of life that the gay and ridiculous phases of existence received, it is true, but little public recognition, or at least but little literary expression. Nathaniel Ward's *Simple Cobbler* appeared in 1647. In 1666 a Virginia colonist, George Alsop (1638-?), published in London a little volume entitled *A Character of the Province of Maryland.* Here again we find a rather successful effort to be humorous.

GEORGE ALSOP

Alsop, who had come over in 1658 and had worked for four years in Baltimore county, Maryland, had seen in the new land much of a surprising nature, and here and there throughout his book are bits of description with the

snap and originality of view that mark a man
of wit. Hear of the good old days in Maryland:

"Here if the lawyer had nothing else to
maintain him but his howling, he might button
up his chaps, and burn his buckram bag, or else
hang it upon a pin until its antiquity had eaten
it up with dirt and dust. Then with a spade,
like his Grandsire Adam, turn up the face of
Creation, purchasing his bread by the sweat
of his brows, that before was got by the motion-
ated water-works of his jaws. . . . All villainous
outrages that are committed in other States,
are not so much as known here. A man may
walk in the open woods as secure from being
externally dissected as in his own house or
dwelling."

We can easily perceive how conscious was
Alsop's effort to be witty. There is a certain
glibness in it all, a wish to glitter, a desire to
put thoughts in eye-catching phrases. Maryland girls, he says, are rather bashful but have
much common-sense. "All complimental
courtships, dressed up in critical rareties, are
mere strangers to them, plain wit comes near-
est their genius; so that he that intends to

court a Mary-Land girl must have something
more than the tautologies of a long winded
speech to carry on his design, or else he may
(for aught I know) fall under the contempt of
her frown and his own windy oration.''

Moses Coit Tyler has declared in his *History
of American Literature* that '' there was but
one American book (*The Simple Cobbler*) produced in the seventeenth century that for
mirthful, grotesque, and slashing energy, can
compare with this.'' The volume is full of
'' wild nonsense.'' In dedicating the work to
Lord Baltimore, Alsop remarks to Maryland
merchants, '' This dish of discourse was intended for you at first, but it was manners to
let my Lord have the first cut, the pie being
his.'' And then, in bidding his little book farewell, he exclaims:

'' Good Fate protect thee from a critic's power;

. . . .

For if they once but wring and screw their mouth,
Cock up their hats, and set the point due-South,
Arms all akimbo, and with belly strut
As if they had Parnassus in their gut,
These are the symptoms of the murthering fall
Of my poor infant, and his burial.''

You will note that there is a touch of sarcasm in this Marylander's humor. And he is not lacking in another trait of piquant humor,— the vigorous use of figures of speech. "The Indians," he tells us, "paint upon their faces one stroke of red, another of green, another of white, and another of black, so that when they have accomplished the equipage of their countenance in this trim, they are *the only Hieroglyphicks and Representatives of the Furies.*"

To construct an elaborate and dignified expression concerning a very simple matter is an old trick among humorists; and our colonial friend by no means forgets it. Describing the decidedly unhumorous procedure of scalping, he remarks that some chosen one from among the Indians "disrobeth the head of skin and hair at one pull, leaving the skull almost as bare as those Monumental Skeletons at Chirurgeons' Hall; but for fear they should get cold by leaving so warm and customary a cap off, they immediately apply to the skull a cataplasm of hot embers to keep their pericranium warm." The volume has many a round-about expression of such a nature. "I have ventured," says he, "to come abroad in print, and if I should be laughed at for my good meaning, it would so break the credit of my understanding that I should never dare to show my face upon the Exchange of conceited wits again."

Your boisterous humorist seems to have flourished at this period far better in the Southern colonies than in the Northern. The " Simple Cobbler " had certain theological pegs which he felt duty-bound to drive into the tough New England sole, and therefore he would fain be witty. But John Pory, when he described the strange customs of "James City," and George Alsop, when he sent forth his " dish of discourse," cared naught for theology; each wrote because the fun was in him. A little later, however, we shall find the case rather reversed; for the times soon called for sarcastic men, for satirists who could turn the laugh on the enemy; and then New England wit flourished with surprising richness.

The great majority of our American humorists have dealt in prose only; but now and then there has come among us a rhyming jester, such as a Leland, a Field, or a Riley, to add melody to laughter. There was no dearth of would-be poets in the early colonial days, and though most of them hobbled rather than soared, we find the very lameness of their poetic feet of more entertainment perhaps than the nimble efforts of some of their successors in the field of American poetry. Not that these dignified divines wished to be entertaining; they were too much in earnest for that. Old Nicholas Noyes of Salem, for instance, was doubtless sorrowing deeply when he wrote of his deceased fellow-preacher:

" For rich array cared not a fig,
  And wore Elisha's periwig;
  At ninety-three had comely face
  Adorned with majesty and grace;
  Before he went among the dead,
  He children's children's children had."

EBENEZER COOK

But here and there was a poetizer intentionally funny, and one of the earliest of these was a certain Ebenezer Cook of Maryland. Cook must have been very much ashamed of his verses, for he has left scarcely a trace of a record about himself. We know simply that he dwelt in Maryland and published in London in 1708 a little book entitled *The Sot Weed Fac-*

tor; or a Voyage to Maryland,—a satire in which is described the laws, government, courts, and constitutions of the country, and also the buildings, feasts, frolics, entertainments, and drunken humors of the inhabitants in that part of America. An eighteenth century title meant a good day's work for the author.

It is chiefly for the edification of " Maryland, my Maryland " that Cook's troubles are aired in this volume. The poet decides to take merchandise to Maryland to trade for tobacco, and he begins the long and tedious voyage.

> " Freighted with fools, from Plymouth sound
>   To Maryland our ship was bound."

Having landed, he opens his store and the " sot-weed factors " crowd about him. " Sotweed," be it known, is " tobacco." Behold these primitive Americans:

> " With neither stockings, hat nor shoe,
>   These sot-weed planters crowd the shore,
>   In hue as tawny as a Moor;
>   Figures so strange, no god designed
>   To be a part of human kind;
>   But wanton nature, void of rest,
>   Moulded the brittle clay in jest."

In the course of his trading Cook meets a
Quaker. Now, evidently Cook is not an admirer of the Quaker sect; else his own words
are deceiving:

> " While riding near a sandy bay,
> I met a Quaker, yea and nay;
> A pious, conscientious rogue
> As e'er wore bonnet or a brogue;
> Who neither swore nor kept his word,
> But cheated in the fear of God;
> And when his debts he would not pay,
> By Light within he ran away."

And by this pious gentleman he is so badly
swindled that he has scarcely anything left to
call his own. When a man is once fooled, he
immediately makes himself a bigger fool by
going to law about it. Ebenezer Cook was no
exception. He found a lawyer who

> " . . . with a stock of impudence,
> Supplied his want of wit and sense;
> With looks demure amazing people;
> No wiser than a daw in steeple "

and who for a liberal fee would

> " . . . have poisoned half the parish,
> And hanged his father on a tree."

Up to Annapolis they go. And see Annapolis in all its primitive beauty!

> "A city situated on a plain,
> Where scarce a house will keep out rain,
>
> . . . .
>
> But stranger here will scarcely meet
> With market-place, exchange, or street.
>
> . . . .
>
> Now here the judges try the suit
> And lawyers twice a year dispute.
> As oft the bench most gravely meet,
> Some to get drunk and some to eat
> A swingling share of country treat."

But the " bench " and the lawyers did something more than consume hearty country fare; the " treat " simply refreshed them for the oratorical battle to come. Hear Cook's own description of this early scene of judicial dignity:

> " We sat like others on the ground,
> Carousing punch in open air,
> Till crier did the court declare.
> The planting rabble being met,
> Their drunken worships being likewise set,
> Crier proclaims that noise should cease,
> And straight the lawyers break the peace.

Wrangling for plaintiff and defendant,
I thought they ne'er would make an end on't,
With nonsense, stuff, and false quotations,
With brazen lies and allegations;
And in the splitting of the cause,
They used such motions with their paws,
As showed their zeal was strongly bent
In blows to end the argument."

Thus the disgusted Ebenezer continues through twenty-one quarto pages. The verse is for the most part the merest doggerel; the humor is of the slam-bang variety; but the fact remains that here was a joker who laughed loudly and had no theological scruples about it. It indicates the development of a national trait, —the irreverent tendency to poke fun on all occasions and at all things no matter how dignified or how honored. Thus, in spite of religious dogma, pioneer hardships, struggles with savage nature and still more savage men, the founders of the Commonwealth developed, perhaps for the most part unconsciously, that most characteristic of our traits—the ability to enjoy the ridiculous.

III

As we look at the cold, stern portraits of the Puritan fathers or read their strict statutes and closely argued theological tracts, we can easily imagine how reluctant the times were to admit to "New Canaan" such a light-minded being as a joker. Yet, there was laughter in spite of these long-faced latter-day saints, and to-day we sometimes laugh *because* of them. The *Bay Psalm Book,* in spite of its good intentions, compels a smile now and then, and that classic the *New England Primer* made even the school boys of colonial days laugh. It is said that after the last alphabetical rhyme, the one illustrating *Z*, of course—

> "Zachias, he climbed a tree
> His Lord to see "—

irreverent New England boys were wont to write:

> "Zachias, he had a fall
> And didn't see his Lord at all!"

43

But too often, as the school lads grew into manhood, they lost that sense of humor which throughout all history has distinguished a broad-minded man from a bigoted zealot.

In the Southern colonies we might reasonably expect a different condition. Here were the descendants of Cavaliers; here was a more liberal religion or, in some sections, none at all. The soil was rich, and life was not harsh. The people loved sports and were fond of show. As early as 1700, according to the Scotch-Carolinian John Lawson, in his *History of Carolina,* the city of Charleston, South Carolina, had " great additions of beautiful large brick buildings," and a well-trained militia whose " officers, both infantry and cavalry, generally appear in scarlet mountings and as rich as in most regiments belonging to the crown, which shows the richness and grandeur of the colony." By 1716 this city and Williamsburg, Virginia, were seeing English comedies played by English troupes, and Williamsburg had a house built for the purpose. Psalm-singing was not then and never has been highly popular in Virginia and the Carolinas; but that there was some demand for real music may be

intimated from the fact that among the effects
of a Virginia musician dying in 1775 there were
such works as Handel's *Acis and Galatea* and
Apollo's Feast and several Corelli pieces.
Among such people we should expect to find a
vein of wit and humor. And doubtless there
was; but what chance would it have had for
publication in the isolated plantation life of the
seventeenth and eighteenth century? Only oc-
casionally do we see the glitter of sparkling wit
or hear the laugh of whole-hearted humor.

WILLIAM BYRD

Among the few who dared to write down
their smiles in those early days there was a
Virginian who undoubtedly had a real genius
for wit,—the versatile Colonel William Byrd
(1674-1744). Moses Coit Tyler in all his
studies of colonial literature seems inclined to
consider him the most brilliant colonist before
the days of Jefferson. How many things he
could do well! How widely, how variously he
touched life!

Born on his father's vast estate, " Westover," Virginia, he was reared with every advantage that wealth, travel, study, and natural

ability could offer. He was a student in England, Holland, and France, was admitted to the bar in the Middle Temple, was chosen a Fellow of the Royal Society, was appointed receiver-general of revenues for Virginia, and upon his return to America at once became a leader in all the colonial movements of his day. For thirty-seven years a member of the Virginia council, he at length became its president, was three times special envoy to England, founded the cities of Richmond and Petersburg, Virginia, gathered the largest and most valuable library in the American colonies, wrote some of the most sprightly and entertaining prose in early American literature, and was, as his epitaph declares, " the constant enemy of all exorbitant power, and hearty friend to the liberties of his country."

In such a man, who had lived so fully and gladly, we should expect to find the glint of wit. And it is here in undeniable brilliancy. With it, too, is a style like the man; for, as Professor Trent has said, in his *Southern Writers*, " as an easy and charming author he is unsurpassed by any other early American save Benjamin Franklin." Shrewd and seri-

ous on occasions, just as much so as Franklin
could be, he at the same time, like Poor Richard, possessed for every trial the saving grace
of humor. Byrd is especially witty when describing North Carolinians. If one is not a
"tar heel," one may enjoy immensely these remarks of the genial Virginian. In 1729 Byrd
was requested to survey the boundary line between Virginia and North Carolina, and after
sixteen weeks spent in this work he wrote all
about it in his highly instructive and highly sarcastic *History of the Dividing Line.* Henceforth the jovial Colonel could not approach any
subject pertaining to North Carolina without
cracking jokes. It reminds one of Artemus
Ward and the Mormons. In 1732 he visited
his mineral land in the Old North State, and
the result was his *Progress to the Mines,* and
the following year another visit brought forth
his *Journey to the Land of Eden.* The sarcasm
of the title is sufficiently plain, I trust.

Evidently Byrd is surprised at conditions in
this wilderness. The only people, he declares,
who have no religion are the Hottentots of the
Cape of Good Hope and of North Carolina!
"They are not troubled with any religious

fumes, and have the least superstition of any
people living. They do not know Sunday from
any other day, any more than Robinson Cru-
soe did; which would give them a great advantage, were they given to be industrious. But
they keep so many Sabbaths every week, that
their disregard of the seventh day has no manner of cruelty in it, either to servant or cattle." North Carolina has " a climate where
no clergyman can breathe, any more than
spiders in Ireland." The town of Edenton,
which Byrd visited, struck him as being unique.
" I believe this is the only metropolis in the
Christian or Mahometan world, where there is
neither church, chapel, mosque, synagogue, or
any other place of public worship whatsoever.
. . . The people seem easy without a minister,
as long as they are exempted from paying
him."

Byrd intimates that these Carolinians had
one supreme virtue in which modern Americans
are sadly deficient; they were not extravagant.
" A citizen here is counted extravagant if he
has ambition enough to aspire to a brick-chim-
ney! " Here good things and hard-earned
cash are never wasted; for the people " are

never guilty of the sin of suffering " liquor " to sour upon their hands," and " they pay no tribute, either to God or to Cæsar." Then, too, their towns are not infested with swarms of daintily dressed dudes; indeed the natives dressed with extreme plainness. Let Byrd tell us of one country gentleman that he met in the South Shore district of the colony: " Like the ravens, he neither ploughed nor sowed, but subsisted chiefly upon oysters which his hand-maid made a shift to gather from the adjacent rocks. Sometimes, too, for change of diet, he sent her to drive up the neighbors' cows, to moisten their mouths with a little milk. But as for raiment, he depended mostly upon the length of beard, and she upon the length of hair, part of which she brought decently for-ward, and the rest dangled behind quite down to her rump, like one of Herodotus's East Indian Pigmies."

It was well for William Byrd that these vari-ous complimentary accounts were not published during his life-time; else the Old North State would doubtless have protested vigorously against that portion of his epitaph that declares him the " hearty friend to the *liberties* of his country.'' These papers, written during the period between 1728 and 1736, were not printed until 1841, when they appeared under the title, *The Westover Manuscripts*. This and the later edition, known as *The Byrd Manuscripts* (1866), came as a surprise to students of American literature; for here was a collection of essays, descriptions, and narratives, brim full of individuality, frothy with wit, and yet lacking none of the red wine of that experience which only active life can bring. Though undoubtedly written mainly for self-enjoyment, the sketches have a style scarcely equalled by any other colonial writers save Franklin and Jefferson, and though lacking the quantity of the works of either of these statesmen, they have a sure lightness of touch never attained by the one and a straightforwardness of expression never indulged in by the other. If he had chosen to remain in England, he would have become undoubtedly one of the greater wits of the eighteenth century; as he did not choose to do so, his fame in his own land was long under a cloud. But there are signs that his '' great elegancy of taste and life '' (to quote from his tombstone) and his merit as a ''well-bred gen-

tleman and polite companion '' will in time receive their deserved recognition. Within the
last decade he has reached that stage where the
school text-books on American literature mention him as '' among others present.''

From the one standpoint of mere individuality and uniqueness of expression this is nothing
more than justice. He has that much sought-
for genius for saying things in a way which is
laughably novel. Of '' ginseng '' he declares:
'' It cheers the heart even of a man that has a
bad wife. . . . 'Tis friendly to the lungs, much
more than scolding itself. . . . It will make a
man live a great while, and very well while he
does live.'' He notices that the path leading
to a certain preacher's door was '' as narrow
as that which leads to heaven, but much more
dirty.'' He remarks on '' the Carolina
felicity of having nothing to do.'' His mills
in that colony, he declares, he found '' as still
for the want of water, as a dead woman's
tongue for the want of breath.'' The noisiest,
most struggling stream he found in the section
he named '' Matrimony Creek.''

Here, then, was an early American of genuine wit. His mind worked quickly; he saw

51

things in novel and surprising relations; he expressed himself with a " snap " and accuracy worthy of imitation even in our own electrical, abbreviated day. One of the earliest of our long list of American humorists, he bears comparison with our latest; for the sparkle of his wit is not a reflection caught from his library, but a light found by his sharp eyes in daily intercourse with his little world of men.

IV

MATHER BYLES

There were once in eighteenth century Boston-town two witty rhymesters who caused more merriment in that staid city than all the other townsmen together. They were named Mather Byles and Joseph Green. Both were brilliant speakers, "profound" scholars, and stern-faced Christians—on Sunday. During the remainder of the week they were such chronic jokers that of one it was written,

" There's punning Byles provokes our smiles,
    A man of stately parts,
He visits folks to crack his jokes,
    Which never mend their hearts.

" With strutting gate and wig so great,
    He walks along the streets;
And throws out wit, or what's like it,
    To every one he meets."

while for the other a friend wrote an epitaph no less suggestive:

" Siste Viator, here lies one
Whose life was whim, whose soul was pun,
And if you go too near his hearse
He'll joke you, both in prose and verse."

Their lives did not flow in unruffled calm
either, as one might suppose in the case of such
merry punsters. Heavy trials came to them;
both died practically exiled by their fellow
countrymen; but both laughed dull care away,
and saw in each tribulation a new cause for a
joke.

Byles was born at Boston in 1706 and could
boast of such ancestors as Richard Mather and
John Cotton. With such forefathers it is a
miracle that he even knew the meaning of a
jest! Educated at Harvard, he became the pastor of Hollis Street Church in his native city in
1733, and there entered into a career which
became a part of the very woof and fibre of
Boston. For forty-three years he preached
sermons "calculated" (pardon the American-
ism) to thrill the most stolid souls, and for
forty-three years he cracked jokes calculated
to upset the gravity of the most long-faced
Puritan; and then at length came a blow that
would have crushed a less stalwart spirit. The

54

Revolution was at hand; Byles declared in favor of Great Britain; and he poured salt on Yankee wounds by praying in public for the health and prosperity of His Majesty King George! But a day of retribution was coming. In 1776, immediately after the evacuation of Boston, a committee of Churchmen was appointed to call the free-speaking parson to task for this unbecoming conduct, and forthwith the charges against him were committed to writing, and the old preacher summoned to the church to answer the accusations.

Now there was no small dread of their sharp-eyed and sharper-tongued pastor—for his was a lofty figure with a fearless look of authority about it—and before he arrived at the meeting the abashed committee had taken seats in a high gallery as distant as possible from the altar. " At length Dr. Byles entered dressed in his ample, flowing robes and bands, under a full bush-wig that had been recently powdered, surmounted by a large three-cornered hat." He walked solemnly to the pulpit, hung his hat upon a peg, seated himself, and waited for developments. The trembling committee could not speak. After a silence of some min-

utes he "turned with a portentous air toward
the gallery," and said, " If ye have aught to
communicate, say on." Here one of the committee, " a very little man with a very little
voice," stood up and began to read:

" The Church of Christ in Hollis Street——"
" Louder! " roared the preacher.
" The Church of Christ in Hollis Street——"
" Louder! " again roared the grim clergy-
man.

The spokesman made a mighty effort and was
allowed to read four or five lines, when the
infuriated pastor arose and thundered,

" 'Tis false! 'Tis false! 'Tis false! And
the Church of Christ in Hollis Street knows
that 'tis false."

Taking down his hat, he marched from the
church and never preached in it again.

In 1777 he was tried in a Boston court for
praying for King George and for helping British soldiers, and was sentenced to imprisonment in a guard-ship and to be exiled to England. Even under these circumstances his
jovial nature did not forsake him; for, upon
being invited to warm himself when first en-
tering the court-room, he exclaimed, " Gentlemen, when I came among you, I expected per-

secution, but I could not think you would have offered me the fire so suddenly!" Again, when his sentence was afterwards changed to imprisonment within his own premises, having sent his guard on an errand, he amused a great crowd of Bostonians by gravely marching, gun in hand, back and forward before his own door, *keeping guard over himself!* Later the watchman was removed, but within a short time was replaced, and then again removed; and the doctor smilingly remarked that he had been " guarded, reguarded, and disreguarded."

On no occasion was he ever known to be without a witty observation. In 1780 a famous " dark day " occurred, and a lady, having sent her child to Byles to ask the cause, received the reply that he was as much in the dark as she was. One day a carriage containing two members of the town-council stuck in a mud-hole in front of his house. The parson gazed for some moments upon the spectacle, and then calmly remarked, " Gentlemen, I have often complained to you of this nuisance, without any attention being paid to it, and I am very glad to see you *stirring in this matter now!* " On one occasion he admitted himself beaten—and that by a woman. For some time he had courted her, but finally she married a suitor named Quincy.

"So, madam," said Byles, "it appears you prefer a Quincy to Byles."

"Yes," replied the lady sharply, "for if there had been anything worse than *biles*, God would have afflicted Job with them!"

JOSEPH GREEN

Now Mather Byles' only equal in wit in the whole city of Boston was his neighbor, Joseph Green. He was indeed a worthy rival. Born at Boston in 1706, and educated at Harvard, he had early become wealthy as a distiller, and had thus gained leisure to produce several amusing and highly popular poems. One of these, long read by New England fire-sides, was his *Entertainment for a Winter's Evening,* a sarcastic account of a boisterous Masonic meeting held in a church.

> "O Muse renown'd for story-telling,
> Fair Clio, leave thy airy dwelling.
>
> .   .   .   .
>
> Come, goddess, and our ears regale
> With a diverting Christmas tale.
> O come, and in thy verse declare

Who were the men and what they were,
And what their names, and what their fame,
And what the cause for which they came
To house of God from house of ale,
And how the parson told his tale:
How they return'd, in manner odd,
To house of ale from house of God.

. . . .

So good Saint Francis, man of grace,
Himself preached to the braying race;
And farther, as the story passes,
He addressed them thus—' My brother asses '."

Another of his successful poems was *A Mournful Lamentation over the Death of Mr. Old Tenor,* the corpse being not a musician, but a species of currency which the government had withdrawn from circulation. These verses made the rough beams of many an ancient farmhouse ring with laughter.

Like Byles, he could furnish laughter on a moment's notice and for all occasions. Seeing workmen tearing down a Boston schoolhouse to make room for an addition to a church, he instantly remarked,

" ' A fig for your learning! I tell you the town,
To make the church larger, must pull the school
down.'

' Unluckily spoken,' replied Master Birch:
' Then learning, I fear, stops the growth of the
church '.' "

The uninspired citizens of Boston wondered
at the intellect that could grind out poetry in
such short order, and make it so amusing besides. Green and his rival wit were the pride
of the town—beings capable of performing
astonishing literary feats.

But the greatest feat of Green's was his
parody on Byles' *Hymn Written during a Voyage*. The wit contest that arose from it gave
old Boston entertainment for weeks. It all
happened after this wise: Dr. Byles was considered such good company that Governor
Belcher of Massachusetts, when starting on a
sea-voyage, enticed him aboard and sailed away
while the parson was taking a glass in the cabin.
When Byles came forth he was surprised to find
" water, water everywhere "; but he took the
joke as a joker should, and prepared to act as
chaplain of the crew. When Sunday came he
found not a single hymn-book on board! Many
a parson would have called it " unkind provi-
dence "; but Byles, being a Boston parson, rose

to the occasion and wrote a hymn that was not at all bad.

" Great God, thy works our wonder raise;
   To thee, our swelling notes belong;
  While skies and winds and rocks and seas,
   Around shall echo to our song.

" Thy power produced this mighty frame,
   Aloud to thee the tempests roar,
Or softer breezes tune thy name
   Gently along the shelly shore.

" Round thee the scaly nation roves,
   Thy opening hands their joys bestow,
Through all the blushing coral groves,
   Those silent gay retreats below.''

.   .   .   .

This was Green's opportunity. Immediately upon publication of Byles' sacred song, he put forth a parody:

" In David's Psalms an oversight
   Byles found one morning at his tea,
Alas! that he should never write
   A proper psalm to sing at sea.

.   .   .   .

" He sat awhile and stroked his muse,
   Then taking up his tuneful pen
Wrote a few stanzas for the use
   Of his seafaring brethren.

The Psalm

" With vast amazement we survey
 The wonders of the deep,
 Where mackerel swim, and porpoise play,
 And crabs and lobsters creep.

" Fish of all kinds inhabit here,
 And throng the dark abode,
 Here haddock, hake, and flounders are,
 And eels, and perch, and cod.

" From waging winds and tempests free
 So smoothly as we pass,
 The shining surface seems to be
 A piece of Bristol glass.

" But when the winds and tempests rise,
 And foaming billows swell,
 The vessel mounts above the skies,
 And lower sinks than hell.

" Our heads the tottering motion feel
 And quickly we become
 Giddy as new-dropp'd calves and reel
 Like Indians drunk with rum."

. . . .

Of course Byles could not suffer this in silence. He replied with a parody on the parody, and Boston had another laugh.

" In Byles' works an oversight
    Green spy'd, as once he smok'd his chunk,
Alas! that Byles should never write
    A song to sing when folks are drunk.

" Thus in the chimney on his block,
    Ambition fir'd the 'stiller's pate;
He summon'd all his little stock,
    The poet's volume to complete.

    .   .   .   .   .   .

Song

" With vast amazement we survey
    The can so broad, so deep,
Where punch succeeds the strong sangree,
    Both to delightful flip.

    .   .   .   .   .   .

" From cruel thoughts and conscience free,
    From dram to dram we pass:
Our cheeks, like apples, ruddy be:
    Our eyeballs look like glass.

    .   .   .   .   .   .

" Thus lost in deep tranquillity,
    We sit, supine and sot,
Till we two moons distinctly see—
    Come, give us t'other pot. "

Thus these two wits amused old-time Boston. It must not be thought, however, that they were continually acting the part of clowns.

The sermons of the one and the serious work of the other, have the gravity, the display of learning, and the untiring length of the best of their species in the eighteenth century, while several of their poems have a sincerity of emotion which surprises us after a reading of their satirical efforts. But if Byles and Green are remembered at all to-day it is because they joked with such tireless enthusiasm. For they proved, unconsciously perhaps, that the winter of Puritanical austerity was passing away and that the summer of laughter, with old Ben Franklin leading the fearless choir of jokers, was almost at hand.

V

WILLIAM DOUGLASS

One of the keenest intellects in America in
the early eighteenth century was that of Dr.
William Douglass (1691-1752) of Boston. His
was a merciless wit, a caustic sarcasm that
spared no man nor movement he thought
tainted with hypocrisy; and the quarrels this
led him into with every undesirable citizen,
from quacks to governors, were most numerous,
and most delightful—to him. Concerning the
physicians of America he presented the following admiring sentiments in his *Summary of
the British Settlements:* " In our plantation
a practitioner, bold, rash, impudent, a liar,
basely born, and educated, has much the advantage of an honest, cautious, modest gentleman. . . . Our American practitioners are so
rash and officious the saying in . . . Ecclesias-
ticus . . . may with much propriety be applied
to them: ' He that sinneth before his Maker,
let him fall into the hand of the physician.'
Frequently there is more danger from the

physician than from the distemper. . . . When
I first arrived in New England, I asked . . . a
noted facetious practitioner what was their
general method of practice. He told me their
practice was very uniform: bleeding, vomiting,
blistering, purging, anodyne, and so forth; if
the illness continued there was ' repetendi '
and finally ' murderandi '." Douglass declared that after an earthquake in Jamaica,
one quack advertised " pills to prevent persons
or their effects suffering by earthquakes."

Individuals were no more spared than general classes of fakes. George Whitefield, he
maintained, was " an insignificant person, of
no general learning, void of common prudence.
. . . The strength of his argument lay in his
lungs. . . . He and his disciples seemed to be
great promoters of impulses, ecstasies, and
wantonness between the sexes. Hypocritical
professions, vociferations, and itineracies are
devotional quackery." In short, he thought
it a great waste of time for the mechanics and
farmers to be gathering to hear such talk; and
he took pleasure in pointing out that every time
the preacher held a meeting, labor was lost
amounting to one thousand pounds.

NATHANIEL AMES

Douglass might well have quoted the words of his contemporary, the shrewd almanac maker, Dr. Nathaniel Ames: " He that lives by fraud is in danger of dying a knave." There was something very much akin in the self-confidence, the shrewdness, and the ready wit of these two Massachusetts physicians. Nathaniel Ames (1708-1764), as both doctor and innkeeper, became learned, not in books but in human nature, and his *Astronomical Diary and Almanac,* so immensely popular throughout all New England, contained the shrewd and tactful wisdom of a man of the world. Current events received full justice in the spare spaces between his astronomical calculations; homely advice to fops, broilers, flirts, and scamps was presented liberally; while absurd prophecies sprinkled here and there, made the rafters of many an ancient farmhouse echo laughter. Thus:

May 22. " Some materials about this time are hatched for the clergy to debate on."

November 9. " These aspects show violent winds and in winter storms of driving snow; mischiefs by the Indians, if no peace; and among us, feuds, quarrels, bloody-noses, broken pates—if not necks."

December 15.

" This cold, uncomfortable weather
Makes Jack and Gill lie close together."

February 24-27. " If you fall into misfortunes, creep through those bushes which have the least briers."

July 16-27. " Every man carries a fool in his sleeve; with some he appears bold, with some he only pops out now and then, but the wise keep him hid."

September 12-16. " To some men their country is their shame; and some are the shame of their country."

This was the sort of reading indeed most needed in the days of Ames and Franklin. Among the wealthier classes of Eastern cities there was a tendency to imitate French customs and to some extent, French vices, a shamefacedness toward the plain and honest ways of the forefathers, and Nathaniel Ames and " Poor Richard," with their almanacs, read in many homes where no other print save that of the Bible was ever seen, had a steadying effect upon the common folk. " I don't pretend to direct the learned; the rich and voluptuous will scorn my direction, and sneer or rail at any

that would reclaim them; but since this sheet
enters the solitary dwellings of the poor and
illiterate, where the studied ingenuity of the
learned writer never comes, if these brief hints
do good, it will rejoice the heart of your humble servant, Nathaniel Ames." His was a
lowly philosophy, intended for the lowly people, where, as he says, " if there was less de-
bating and more acting, 'twould be better
times; " for

> " The lawyers' tongues—they never freeze,
> If warmed with honest clients' fees."

Numerous writers have said that Ben
Franklin was the first man ever to have published an almanac filled with information, wit,
and philosophy; but eight years before the
" Poor Richard " sayings began to delight both
America and Europe, Nathaniel Ames had prepared the readers for just such a class of literature and had made possible the enormous
success which was to come in this manner to
him whom we shall next discuss,—Benjamin
Franklin.

VI

BENJAMIN FRANKLIN

If Abe Lincoln and Zeb Vance and Davy Crockett had done and said all the funny things they have been credited with, they would have been busy at nothing else for some centuries. It is the good fortune, or perhaps, the fate, of every conspicuous character to gather about his memory a folk lore, doubtless full of admiration, but not always flattering in its good taste and morality. One of the earliest of these American heroes was that genial humorist, philosopher, scientist, statesman, editor, and common-sense man, Benjamin Franklin. The jokes and shrewd sayings attributed to this prince of good fellows would fill a bulky volume. Gradually there has gathered about him a host of tales until in truth he has become at length the central figure in a lengthy myth or comic epic.

The chief incidents in Ben Franklin's life are

so well known to every intelligent American
that it seems unnecessary at this time to enter
into any lengthy recital of them. A genuine
man and a lover of genuine men, he seems to
interest every class of people. Perhaps no
other early American, save Jefferson, touched
life at so many points. Let us, for a moment,
refresh our memory of his manifold experi-
ences. Born at Boston, January 17, 1706, the
son of a candle-maker and soap-boiler, he very
early learned the full meaning of toil; for at
the age of ten he was hard at work in his
father's shop. He was a strong boy with a
solid, prudent mind; but he chafed under the
confinement and drudgery of his father's occupation, and, like many a youngster of spirit,
longed to escape a commonplace life by running
off to sea.

His saving grace, however, was his fondness
for reading, and on books he spent all that he
obtained as a child-laborer. Very serious volumes he read, too; for he tells us that the first
book he bought, *Pilgrim's Progress,* was sold to
buy Burton's *Historical Collection*, and that
among the other books of his youthful library
were Plutarch's *Lives* and Mather's *Essay to*

do Good. He early had an itching to write poetry; but this was cured by his father's blunt statement that poets were generally beggars, and doubtless, judging by the specimens which matter-of-fact Ben has left behind, the advice was excellent; for he would indeed have been a beggar had he received his poetic dues. His constant reading, however, prompted him to improve his prose style, and by untiring practice with the *Spectator* as a model, he developed a simplicity and a directness of expression not excelled by many writers in the English language.

We may not linger over the details of his boyhood struggles. At the age of twelve he was apprenticed to his brother, James, publisher of *The New England Courant* of Boston, caught what Holmes has called "lead-poisoning," or the desire to appear in print, and contributed anonymous articles to the *Courant*. At seventeen he had run away to Philadelphia, where his ramble with a loaf of bread at his mouth and one under each arm amused his future wife, and where his taking a good nap in the Quaker meeting-house indicated his future complaisancy toward all religion. The next important step occurred when, after being sent to England by a deceitful politician to purchase a printing outfit, he found himself stranded in London and obliged to seek work in a metropolitan printing-house. A great man forces luck from his adversities; and we find Franklin shrewdly gaining an accurate knowledge of every detail of the art of printing. When, after eighteen months' absence, he returned to America, no other man in the country could approach him in typographical skill and fertility of resources.

By 1729 he had " set up " shop for himself, and then what a wonderful career of activity began! He established *The Pennsylvania Gazette,* founded the famous Junto Club, created the first subscription-library in America, began the publication of *Poor Richard's Almanac* in 1732, was clerk of the General Assembly in 1736, postmaster of Philadelphia in 1737, and postmaster-general for the American colonies in 1753, organized the first American police force supported by taxation, the first fire-company in Philadelphia, and the State militia of Pennsylvania, founded the University of Pennsylvania, discovered the identity of

lightning and electricity in 1752, was awarded
the Copley medal in 1753, was chosen a Fellow
of the Royal Society, was a delegate to the
Albany Convention of 1754, and there proposed
a plan for a union of the colonies, was representative of Pennsylvania in England from
1757 to 1762, was colonial representative to
oppose the Stamp Act of 1764, was European
representative of various colonies until 1775,
was a signer of the Declaration of Independence, was American Ambassador in
France from 1776 until 1785, was the moving
power in procuring the treaty with England
in 1783, was president of Pennsylvania from
1785 to 1788, was a delegate to the Federal
Convention of 1787, and served as a uniting
spirit in that final endeavor to form a nation.
Honors were lavished upon him. Both Yale
and Harvard gave him the M.A. degree; St.
Andrews and Oxford conferred upon him the
Doctor of Laws; Edinburgh presented him the
freedom of the city; London society lionized
him; and France received him with an ovation
greater than that accorded Voltaire. Number-
less medallions in his honor were struck off, and
a Frenchman made the brilliant summary:

" He has seized the lightning from heaven and the scepter from tyrants."

It was a wonderful life, and yet how simple! The man was never puffed up, never vainglorious. Deliberately he had trained himself to be broad-minded; he tossed dogmatism to the winds. In his early manhood he began to refrain from over-positive statements, and in his old age he could say: " Perhaps for the last fifty years no one has ever heard a dogmatical expression escape me." It may be that he was a trifle too shrewd. He seems indeed a little too calculating when he declares, " I took care not only to be *in reality* industrious and frugal, but to avoid the appearances to the contrary. I dressed plain, and was seen at no places of idle diversions. I never went out afishing or shooting; a book, indeed, sometimes debauched me from my work, but that was seldom, was private, and gave no scandal." But, as Sainte-Beuve points out, " there is a flower of religion, a flower of honor, a flower of chivalry that you must not require of Franklin."

From such a man we should expect a sort of shrewd, earthy humor, and, verily, we are not disappointed. In his youthful days he wrote a poem entitled *Paper,* in which he expresses his opinion on poetic matters:

" What are our poets, take them as they fall,
  Good, bad, rich, poor, much read, not read at all?
  Then all their work in the same class you'll find:
  They are the *mere waste paper* of mankind."

But to counterbalance this weakness on the spiritual side, we find in another stanza that blunt common-sense for which he was so noted:

" The retail politician's anxious thought
  Deems this side always right and that stark
      naught;
  He foams with censure, with applause he raves,
  A dupe to rumors and a tool of knaves:
  He'll want no type his weakness to proclaim
  While such a thing as foolscap has a name."

In those busy days of the eighteenth century such a man was needed. His newspaper soon became a power in the land, while *Poor Richard's Almanac*—what might we not say of it and its fame! Begun in 1732, it was issued for twenty-five consecutive years at the rate of ten thousand per year, and very few families in all New England and the neighboring colonies escaped its influence. What a collection of shrewd sayings and proverbs were in those quaint pamphlets! In 1758 Franklin collected the principal statements in one connected discourse, *Father Abraham's Speech,* supposed to be an address given by a wise old gentleman at an auction. The result astonished even the self-possessed author; for the brief lecture was universally applauded. Poor Richard, who was " excessive poor " and whose wife was " excessive proud," has become as much a living figure in literature as Tom Jones or Mr. Pickwick. His common-sense is so extreme that it verges on the ridiculous, and just there is the main point in Franklin's humor. " The poor man must walk to get meat for his stomach, the rich man to get a stomach for his meat." " Silks and satins, scarlet and velvets, put out the kitchen fire." " Three may keep a secret if two of them are dead." " If you would have your business done, go; if not, send." " Keep thy shop, and thy shop will keep thee." " Fish and visitors smell after three days." Any one who can read Father Abraham's harangue without smiling is a dangerous man, fit for treason, spoil, and the other Shakespearian sins.

All of Franklin's humor has a lesson; it is meant to do somebody good—oftentimes himself. Even his practical jokes always were to his own profit. One day he came, half-frozen from his long ride, to a wayside inn. A great crowd was about the fire, and for some time Franklin stood shivering. Suddenly he turned to the hostler.

"Hostler," said he in a loud voice, "have you any oysters?"

"Yes, sir."

"Well, then," commanded Franklin in still louder tones, "give my horse a peck!"

"What!" exclaimed the hostler, "give your horse oysters!"

"Yes," said Franklin, "give him a peck."

The hostler, decidedly astonished, prepared the oysters and started for the stable. Everybody instantly arose from the fire-place and rushed out to see the marvellous horse eat oysters. Franklin took the most comfortable seat before the roaring blaze, and calmly awaited developments. Soon all returned, disappointed and shivering.

"I gave him the oysters, sir," said the hostler, "but he wouldn't eat them."

" Oh, well, then," answered Franklin non-chalantly, " I suppose I shall have to eat them myself. Suppose you try him with a peck of oats."

The other guests took seats wherever they could find any, and there was silence for some time.

His *Autobiography* contains several similar instances of his ability to take care of Benjamin Franklin, Esquire. How narrowly, by the way, we missed not having that book at all! In 1771, while visiting at the home of the Bishop of St. Asaph in Hampshire, England, he wrote a long letter to his son, the governor of New Jersey, telling some of the main incidents of his life. Thirteen years later the letter was swept into a garbage pile in the streets of Philadelphia, but luckily was found by a friend of Franklin's, and was sent to the philosopher with the request that he complete the account. Franklin, then at Passy, France, wrote another chapter, and four years later, at Philadelphia, added other portions and brought the account down to 1757, the year he entered actively into public life. Soon after his death, the story was translated into French, and in 1793 was turned back into English and published in London. In 1817 there was a direct publication of the manuscript; but not until 1868 was there given to the world a complete edition of this highly profitable and entertaining narrative. How much we would have missed—his ridiculous entry into Philadelphia, his conflict between his avarice and George Whitefield's eloquence, his shrewdness in business affairs, his good-humored handling of statesmen.

Franklin must have been a centre of attraction in all assemblies. He had a witty saying ready for every occasion. We all remember how neatly and yet how significantly he answered the member of the Colonial Congress who declared they would all have to hang together. " Yes," rejoined Franklin, " or verily we shall hang separately! " Jefferson, in his biographical sketches, tells how Franklin, noticing his sensitiveness over the mutilation of the *Declaration of Independence,* tried to comfort him by a little story: " When I was a journeyman printer, one of my companions, an apprentice hatter, having served out his time, was about to open shop for himself. His first concern was to have a handsome sign-board, with a proper inscription. He composed it in these words, ' *John Thompson, Hatter, makes and sells hats for ready money,*' with a figure of a hat subjoined; but he thought he would submit it to his friends for their amendments. The first he showed it to thought the word ' Hatter ' tautologous, because followed by the words ' makes hats,' which showed he was a hatter. It was struck out. The next observed that the word ' makes ' might as well be omitted, because his customers would not care who made the hats. If good and to their mind, they would buy, by whomsoever made. He struck it out. A third said he thought the words ' *for ready money* ' were useless, as it was not the custom of the place to sell on credit. . . . They were parted with, and the inscription now stood, ' John Thompson sells hats.' ' *Sells* hats! ' says his next friend. ' Why nobody will expect you to give them away; what then is the use of that word? ' It was stricken out, and ' hats ' followed it the rather as there was one painted on the board. So the inscription was reduced ultimately to ' John Thompson ' with the figure of a hat subjoined.'' Jefferson's heated temper was cooled considerably by the narrative.

John Adams tells us, in his *Diary*, of another story of Franklin's—one that gave the republican French extreme content. "A Spanish writer of certain visions of Hell relates that a certain devil, who was civil and well-bred, showed him all the apartments of the place, among others that of deceased kings. The Spaniard was much pleased at so illustrious a sight, and after viewing them for some time said he should be glad to see the rest of them. ' The rest? ' said the demon. ' Here are all the kings that ever reigned upon earth from the creation of it to this day. What the devil would the man have? ' " It was this ability to tell a joke that tickled some certain weakness in his audience that made him so useful in many a nerve-straining crisis.

He saw life clearly and did not attempt to evade its plain teachings. His advice, while often eccentric in appearance, was always sane. A gouty alderman came to him seeking a cure for the disease.

"Why," said Franklin, "take a bucket of water and a cord of wood three times a week! "

The alderman forgot both his dignity and his gout.

" What! " he exclaimed. " Why, how can I do that? "

" Well," replied Franklin, " drink a cup of the former three times a day and carry the latter up three flights of stairs."

Doubtless the alderman preferred the gout.

Franklin himself was sometimes a sufferer from this aristocratic ailment, and one of his most famous bits of humor is his *Dialogue with the Gout.*

Franklin—Eh! Oh! Eh! What have I done to merit these cruel sufferings?

Gout—Many things; you have ate and drank too freely and too much indulged those legs of yours in their indolence.

Franklin—Who is it that accuses me?

Gout—It is I, even I, the Gout.

.   .   .   .

Franklin—I take—Eh! Oh!—as much exercise— Eh—as I can, Madam Gout. You know my sedentary state, and, on that account, it would seem, Madam Gout, as if you might spare me a little, seeing it is not altogether my own fault.

Gout—Not a jot; your rhetoric and your politeness are thrown away; your apology avails nothing. . . . Why instead of gaining an appetite for breakfast, by salutary exercise, you amuse yourself with books, pamphlets, or newspapers, which commonly are not worth the reading. Yet you eat an inordinate breakfast, four dishes of tea, with cream, and one or two buttered toast, with slices of hung beef, which I fancy are not things the most easily digested. . . . But what is your practice after dinner? Walking in the beautiful gardens of those friends with whom you have dined would be the choice of men of sense; yours is to be fixed down to chess, where you are found engaged for two or three hours! . . . Wrapt in the speculations of this wretched game, you destroy your constitution. . . . The same taste prevails with you in Passy, Auteuil, Montmartre, or Sanoy, places where there are the finest gardens and walks, a pure air, beautiful women and most agreeable and instructive conversation; all which you might enjoy by frequenting the walks. But these are rejected for this abominable game of chess. Fie then, Mr. Franklin! But amidst my instructions I had almost forgot to administer my wholesome corrections; so take that twinge—and that.

Franklin—Oh! Eh! Oh! Ohhh! as much instruction as you please, Madam Gout, and as many reproaches; but pray, Madam, a truce with your corrections.

Gout—No, Sir, no—I will not abate a particle of what is so much for your good,—therefore—

. . . .

Franklin—Your reasoning grows tiresome.

Gout—I stand corrected. I will be silent and continue my office; take that, and that.

Franklin—Oh! Ohh! Talk on, I pray you!

Gout—No, no; I have a good number of twinges for you to-night, and you may be sure of some more to-morrow.

Franklin—What, with such a fever! I shall go distracted. Oh! Eh! Can no one bear it for me?

Gout—Ask that of your horses; they have served you faithfully.

. . . .

Franklin—I am convinced now of the justness of Poor Richard's remark that " our debts and our sins are always greater than we think for."

Gout—So it is. Your philosophers are sages in your maxims and fools in your conduct.

. . . .

Franklin—Ah! how tiresome you are!

Gout—Well, then, to my office; it should not be forgotten that I am your physician. There.

Franklin—Ohh! What a devil of a physician.

Franklin was so extremely busy in the various governmental actions connected with the Revolution that he doubtless did not have time to write as much as other wits of the day in defence of his native land. That he by no means lacked the ability is shown by at least three cunningly phrased and bitterly satirical sketches written by him to show the injustice of the British position. These were his *Rules for Reducing a Great Empire to a Small one* (1773), *An Edict by the King of Prussia* (1773), and a letter of instructions *From the Count de Schaumbergh to the Baron Hohendorf commanding the Hessian Troops in America* (1777).

The first of these tells with a bitterness, all the more effective because of its calmness, just how to destroy a nation. The method, of course, coincides identically with that then being pursued by Great Britain in her dealings with her colonies. Note a few lines from this sarcastic broadside:

" An ancient sage valued himself upon this, that though he could not fiddle, he knew how to make a great city of a little one. The science that I, a modern simpleton, am about to communicate, is the very reverse.

" 1. In the first place, gentlemen, you are to consider that a great empire, like a great cake, is most easily diminished at the edges. Turn your attention, therefore, first to your *remotest* provinces; that, as you get rid of them, the next may follow in order.

" 2. That the possibility of this separation may always exist, take special care the provinces are *never incorporated with the mother country;* that they do

not enjoy the same common rights, the same privileges
in commerce; and that they are governed by severer
laws, all of your enacting, without allowing them any
share in the choice of the legislators.

. . . .

"4. However peaceably your colonies have submitted to your government, shown their affection to
your interests, and patiently borne their grievances,
you are to suppose them *always inclined to revolt,* and
treat them accordingly. Quarter troops upon them,
who by their insolence may provoke the rising of mobs,
and by their bullets and bayonets suppress them. By
this means, like the husband who uses his wife ill from
suspicion, you may in time convert your suspicions
into realities.

. . . .

"7. When such governors have crammed their
coffers, and made themselves so odious to the people
that they can no longer remain among them, with
safety to their persons, *recall and reward* them with
pensions. You may make them baronets too, if that
respectable order should not think fit to resent it.
All this will contribute to encourage new governors in
the same practice, and make the supreme government
detestable."

The second Franklin satire, *An Edict by the
King of Prussia,* caused a great commotion in
England. Couched in diplomatic terms, and

sounding somewhat like other papers by
Frederick the Great, it was taken by numerous
English to be the real article, and great was
their indignation toward the impudent German
ruler. Franklin, noting Great Britain's extensive claims upon the colonies, published in
the *Public Advertiser* an edict by Frederick
making exactly the same claims upon the British Isles. It contained most serious language.
" And all persons in the said island are hereby
cautioned not to oppose in any wise the execution of this, our edict, or any part thereof, such
opposition being high treason; of which all
who are suspected shall be transported in fetters from Britain to Prussia, there to be tried
and executed according to the Prussian Law."
According to Franklin, he himself was present
at an English breakfast table when a guest came
rushing in with the paper, and shouting,
" Here's news for ye! Here's the King of
Prussia claiming a right to this kingdom! "
A few paragraphs were read, and then another
guest burst forth: " Damn his impudence; I
dare say we shall hear by next post that he is
upon his march with one hundred thousand men
to back this! " Later the reader began to dis-

cern the hoax, and, turning to Franklin, said with disgust, " I'll be hanged if this is not some of your American jokes upon us."

The third of Franklin's war satires, Count de Schaumbergh's instructions, deals with that infamous bargain by which princes of Germany sold the bodies and souls of their Hessian subjects to be used by the British king against his own subjects. This is one of the bitterest satires of colonial days; it is indeed too bitter to be amusing. It shows that beneath the calmness of its philosophical author there was the fiery, hating soul of the patriot.

There are a thousand and one anecdotes and jokes of Franklin's that we might hear again with entertainment; but we must leave him and them; for, to use his own words, perhaps we " are paying too much for the whistle." In him we have a genuine specimen of American common-sense, a common-sense so large, even at times so disproportioned, as to appear almost lop-sided and " funny." Yet, in it is that same hidden censure, that disgust for all shams, that standing for honest, even if earthy, ideals which has characterized the great majority of the successors of this pioneer in American humor. And in the words of Bancroft, in his New York Historical Society lecture of December 9, 1852, " Franklin was the greatest diplomatist of the eighteenth century. He never spoke a word too soon; he never spoke a word too late; he never spoke a word too much; he never failed to speak the right word at the right season."

I.

In times of war we may, of course, expect scornful sarcasm and biting satire; and, therefore, as we approach the prolonged struggle of the American Revolution, we find the American sense of the ludicrous becoming more and more alert. The colonist becomes eager to discern the weakness of his enemy, to discover all of that enemy's predicaments, and to set them with taunting laughter before the world. Many were the satirical "take-offs" of the day. They began, not suddenly, but many years before the actual outbreak of war; indeed, we might easily trace the bitterness of feeling through occasional verse back even to Bacon's Rebellion in 1676. But as we draw near the momentous year, 1776, the harvest of satirical sketches and poems is indeed plentiful.

A NARRATIVE OF GEORGIA

In 1740, for instance, three Georgia patriots of Scotch-Irish blood, Patrick Tailfer, Hugh

Anderson, and David Douglas, issued against Governor Oglethorpe a bitter tirade entitled *A True and Historical Narrative of Georgia.* Here is sarcasm enough for any man—even for the greedy Oglethorpe himself. Many countries, declare the three hot-heads, " fondly imagine it necessary to communicate to such young settlements the fullest rights and properties, all the immunities of their mother-countries, and privileges rather more extensive. . . . But your Excellency's concern for our perpetual welfare could never permit you to propose such transitory advantages for us. You considered riches, like a divine and a philosopher, as the *irritamenta malorum,* and knew that they were disposed to inflate weak minds with pride, to hamper the body with luxury, and introduce a long variety of evils. Thus have you ' protected us from ourselves,' as Mr. Waller says, by keeping all earthly comforts from us. You have afforded us the opportunity of arriving at the integrity of the primitive times by entailing a more than primitive poverty on us. . . . The valuable virtue of humility is secured to us by your care to prevent our procuring, or so much as seeing, any negroes . . . lest our simplicity might mistake the poor Africans for greater slaves than ourselves. . . .

> Like Death you reign
> O'er silent subjects and a desert plain."

Under the first flush of war, satires appeared in practically every newspaper in the colonies. Of course, tea soon came in for its full share of sarcasm. One patriotic woman wrote a poem entitled *Virginia Banishing Tea,* containing the lines:

> " Begone, pernicious, baleful Tea,
>   With all Pandora's ills possessed;
>   Hyson, no more beguiled by thee,
>   My noble sons shall be oppressed."

Another hater of British tea and tyranny wrote:

> " Vain, foolish curmudgeons,
>   To think we, like gudgeons,
>   Swallow baits that of Freedom bereaves;
>   Tea, nabobs, and minions,
>   With their dire opinions,
>   May be damned—but we'll not be slaves."

CHRONICLES OF THE TIMES

Perhaps the best of the innumerable sarcastic sketches on the drink was the series of pamphlets entitled *The First Book of the American Chronicles of the Times,* issued in 1774 and 1775. Its mock dignity as a parody on the Bible adds much to its sharp criticisms on British injustice. A few quotations to show its flavor:

" 1. And behold! when the tidings came to the great city that is afar off, the city that is in the land of Britain, how the men of Boston, even the Bostonites, had arose, a great multitude, and destroyed the Tea, the abominable Merchandise of the east and cast it into the midst of the sea,

" 2. That the Lord the King waxed exceeding wroth, insomuch that the form of his visage was changed, and his knees smote one against the other.

" 3. Then he assembled together the Princes, the Nobles, the Counselors, the Judges, and all the Rulers of the people, . . . and when he had told them what things were come to pass,

" 4. They smote their breasts and said, ' These men fear thee not, O King, neither have they obeyed the voice of our Lord the King, nor worshipped the Tea-Chest, which thou has set up. . . .' "

The King, following the advice of his wise men, sends an army, under "Thomas the Gageite," to subdue the Bostonites; but a sorrowful letter from this leader tells of great expectations ruined:

"5. 'O King, thy servant is in a great strait; the men of New England are stiff-necked, and as stubborn hogs, neither knoweth thy servant what to make of them; they are worse unto me than all the plagues of Egypt.

"6. 'For they resolve upon resolves, they address, they complain, they protest, they compliment, they flatter, they sooth and they threatened to root me up.

. . . .

"9. 'For the men of New England are as venomous as the poison of a serpent, even like the deaf adder that stoppeth her ears; they give good words with their mouths, but curse with their hearts; they go to and fro in the evening and grin like a dog, and run about through the city; they slander thy servant, they make a byword of him, and grudge him everything; yet complain if they be not satisfied.

"10. 'Surely, O King, the spirit of Oliver or the devil is got in them.'

. . . .

"36. Now it came to pass, while the Gageites abode in the land of the Bostonites, they day by day committed iniquity; they made great clattering with their sackbuts, their psalteries, their dulcimers, bands of music, and vain parade.

" 37. And they drummed with their drums, and piped with their pipes, making mock fights, and running to and fro like shitepokes on the muddy shore.

" 38. Moreover, by night, they abused the watchmen on duty, and the young children of Boston by the wayside, making mouths at them, calling them Yankees."

Then, at length, says the chronicler, when this condition was no longer bearable, Jeremiah (Samuel Adams) and other prophets of the Americanites spake loud and showed the people how they were about to be compelled to " bow down to the Tea Chest, the God of the Heathen." "And they assembled themselves together, in a Congress in the great city of Philadelphia, in the house of the Carpenters, the builders' house, in the land of Pennsylvania, on the seventh day of the ninth month, with their coaches, their chariots, their camels, their horsemen, and their servants, a great multitude and they communed together."

Thus we have the course of history from the Night of the Tea Chest to the Day of the Declaration.

Such pamphlets and tracts, spread throughout the principal cities and even into the rural districts, of course caused the colonists much merriment, and, in no small degree, contributed to their confidence and to their growing dislike for things British. John Adams says that he found in one home King George's picture standing upside down on the floor, with this inscription attached:

" Behold the man who had it in his power,
  To make a kingdom tremble and adore.
  Intoxicate with folly, see his head
  Placed where the meanest of his subjects tread.
  Like Lucifer, the giddy tyrant fell:
  He lifts his heels to Heaven, but points his head to
    Hell."

After war really began, the satirical squibs came thick and fast. The ridiculous retreat of the British from Concord was the source of many a sarcastic verse, while the Battle of Bunker Hill with its " near-victory " for the Americans gave many a patriotic scribbler an opportunity to show his talent. A few specimens must suffice. Thus, a ballad, widely cir-

culated in the Revolutionary days and supposed to be written by a Yankee-Irishman, was
the one commonly entitled *An Address to the
Troops in Boston:*

AN ADDRESS TO THE TROOPS

" By me faith, but I think ye're all makers of bulls,
    Wid your brains in your breeches, your guts in your
        skulls!
    Get home wid your muskets, and put up your
        swords,
    And look in your books for the meaning of words:
    Ye see now, me honeys, how much ye're mistaken,—
    For Concord by discord can never be baten! "

" How brave ye wint out wid your muskets all bright,
    And thought to befrighten the folks wid the sight;
    But whin ye got there, how they powder'd your
        pums,
    And all the way home how they pepper'd your
        ———;
    And is it not, honeys, a comical crack,

    To be proud in the face, and be shot in the back?

    .   .   .   .

" And what have ye got now, wid all your designin',
    But a town without victuals to sit down and dine
        in;

And to look on the ground like a parcel of noodles,
And sing how the Yankees have conquer't the
    Doodles;
I'm sure if ye're wise, ye'll make peace for a
    dinner—
For fightin' and fastin' will soon make ye thinner.''

Shortly before the Battle of Bunker Hill, when Clinton, Howe and Burgoyne had arrived to end quickly and permanently this petty rebellion of colonial ruffians, there appeared for sale on the streets of the three leading cities, Boston, New York, and Philadelphia, a lively ballad with plenty of ginger and snap, and a world of scorn for British governmental ideas,—*A New Song to an Old Tune.* Tea and taxation, as usual, come in for discussion; as we may see from these few lines:

A NEW SONG

'' There is no knowing where this oppression will
    stop;
Some say—' There's no cure but a capitol chop ';
And that I believe's each American's wish,
Since you've drenched them with tea, and deprived
    'em of fish.

" The birds of the air and the fish of the sea,
    By the gods, for poor Dan Adams' use were made
        free,
    Till a man with more power than old Moses would
        wish,
    Said—' Ye wretches, ye shan't touch a fowl or a
        fish ! '

" Three Generals these mandates have borne cross
        the sea,
    To deprive 'em of fish and to make 'em drink tea;
    In turn, sure, these freemen will boldly agree
    To give 'em a dance upon Liberty Tree."

ANOTHER PROPHECY

One of these generals, Howe, had a good
reputation as a warrior, and at first the patriots
were fearful lest victory might indeed prove
easy for him. The Loyalists knew this, and
one of them, to help along the British cause,
started the report that a prophetic hen at Plymouth had laid an egg bearing upon its shell
the inscription: " Oh, America ! Howe shall be
thy conqueror." But as time dragged on and
Howe's strategic gifts shone with a most dim
lustre, the Americans took heart, and one of
them in turn answered the hen in *Another
Prophecy*, a part of which ran thus:

" When eggs can speak what fools endite,
  And hens can talk as well as write,
  When crocodiles shed honest tears,
  And truth with hypocrites appears;
  When every man becomes a knave
  And feels the spirit of the slave,
  And when veracity again
  Shall in a Tory's bosom reign;
  When vice is virtue, darkness light,
  And freemen are afraid to fight;
  When they forget to play the men
  And with the spirit of a hen
  Desert the just and sacred cause,
  And opening Heaven smiles applause
  On such a bloody, barbarous foe,—
  Then I'll be conquered by a Howe! "

But let us not think for a moment that the renowned Howe received all the broadsides; Burgoyne, Benedict Arnold, and many another enemy of the American cause were handled with justice if not with mercy.

" In seventeen hundred and seventy-seven
  General Burgoyne set out for Heaven;
  But as the Yankees would rebel,
  He missed his route, and went—to Hell! "

And this for Arnold, appearing in the *New Jersey Gazette,* November 1, 1780:

" Quoth Satan to Arnold: ' My worthy good fellow,
  I love you much better than ever I did;
You live like a prince, with Hal * may get mellow,—
  But mind that you both do just what I bid.'

" Quoth Arnold to Satan: ' My friend, do not doubt
      me!
  I will strictly adhere to all your great views;
To you I 'm devoted, with all things about me—
  You 'll permit me, I hope, to die in my shoes.' "

---

* *Hal: Sir. Henry Clinton.*

II

WITHERSPOON'S PARODY

It is interesting to see how many local conflicts of wit resulted from the ill-feeling between Tory and patriot. Many a mocking laugh echoes down from those troubled days. Note, for example, John Witherspoon's parody on James Rivington's petition to Congress. Rivington was a New York printer whose sympathy was decidedly with the British but whose prosperous business was decidedly with the Americans. Accordingly, in May, 1775, he wrote a paper, *A Tory's Petition to the Continental Congress,* in which he endeavored to show his neutrality, promised to give no offence and boasted somewhat of the extensiveness of his business. Rivington was extremely unpopular among the patriots—his office was afterwards mobbed—and many sarcastic commentaries were made upon his petition. It remained for old John Witherspoon, Scotchman, preacher, college-president, and signer of the *Declaration* (pardon the combination!), to voice the sentiments of the people in a widely read parody. It "respectively sheweth—

" That a great part of the British forces has already left this city, and from many symptoms there is reason to suspect that the remainder will speedily follow them. Where they are gone or going is perhaps known to themselves, perhaps not; certainly, however, it is unknown to us, the loyal inhabitants of the place, and other friends of government who have taken refuge in it, and who are therefore filled with distress and terror on the unhappy occasion.

" That as soon as the evacuation is completed, it is more than probable, the city will be taken possession of by the forces of your high mightiness, followed by vast crowds of other persons—Whigs by nature and profession—friends to the liberties and foes to the enemies of America. Above all, it will undoubtedly be filled with shoals of Yankees, that is to say, the natives and inhabitants (or as a great lady in this metropolis generally expresses it, the *wretches*) of New England.

. . . .

" That your petitioner, in particular, is at the greatest loss what to resolve upon or how to shape his course. He has no desire at all, either to be roasted in Florida, or frozen to death in Canada or Nova

Scotia. Being a great lover of fresh cod, he has had thoughts of trying a settlement in Newfoundland, but recollecting that the New England men have almost all the same appetite, he was obliged to relinquish that project entirely. If he should go to Great Britain, dangers no less formidable present themselves. Having been a bankrupt in London, it is not impossible that he might be accommodated with a lodging in Newgate, and that the ordinary there might oblige him to say his prayers, a practice from which he hath had an insuperable aversion all his life long.

.   .   .   .

" I beg leave to suggest that upon being received into favor, I think it would be in my power to serve the United States in several important respects. I believe many of your officers want politeness. They are, like old Cincinnatus, taken from the plough; and therefore must still have a little roughness in their manners and deportment. Now, I myself am the pink of courtesy, a genteel, portly, well-looking fellow as you will see in a summer's day. . . . I hear with pleasure that your people are pretty good scholars, and have made particularly very happy advances in the art of swearing, so essentially necessary to a gentleman. Yet I dare say they will themselves confess, that they are still in this respect far inferior to the English army. There is, by all account, a coarseness and sameness in their expressions; whereas there is variety, sprightliness, and figure in the oaths of gentlemen well educated. . . . I have imported many of the most necessary articles for appearance in genteel life. I can give them Lavornitti's soap-balls to wash their brown hands clean, perfumed gloves, paint, powder, and pomatum. . . .

" Finally, I hope I may be of service to the United States as a writer, publisher, collector, and maker of news. . . . I might write those things only, or chiefly which you wish to be disbelieved, and thus render you the most essential service. . . . It would be endless to mention all my devices; and therefore I will only say further that I can take a truth and so puff and swell and adorn it, still keeping the proportion of its parts, but enlarging their dimensions, that you could hardly discover where the falsehood lay, in case of a strict investigation."

III

TORY SATIRES

The Tory satires that have been handed down to this day are far less numerous and decidedly less talented than similar efforts by the patriots. This may be because the Tories, being in the minority, may have feared to speak with the same recklessness as their opponents; or, perhaps, the better the Tory pamphlets and tracts were, the more quickly and completely they were destroyed by the " Yankees." Moreover, the Loyalists could print their broadsides only in New York or Boston, where the British soldiers were for a time in absolute control. But whatever the Tories' sheets lacked in quantity and genius, they apparently endeavored to make up in epithets, foul language, and an irritating condescension. Moses Coit Tyler in his *Literary History of the American Revolution* gives three reasons for this last characteristic: (1) Loyalists had an unclouded conviction that they themselves were right; (2) they had been accustomed to leading all social and political movements, and therefore considered the Revolution a plebeian enterprise; (3) the Loyalists fully expected Great Britain to win. "Since they could not reason down the rebellion, they meant, not only to fight it down, but to laugh it down, to sneer it down, and to make it seem to all the world as ridiculous as, to themselves, it already seemed sordid and vulgar and weak." Apparently only the most violent " tongue-lashings " would serve for this purpose.

THE PAUSING LOYALIST

Undoubtedly numerous colonists became " patriots " through fear that their property would be confiscated and they themselves be driven into exile. The Congress of 1774 had created a so-called " association " to be assented to by every believer in American liberty. This, of course, the Tories considered a tempting subject for sarcastic consideration, and the few journals which would receive contributions from Britain's friends printed poetic and prose comments that must have enraged the "embattled farmers.'' For instance, the *Middle-sex Journal* of January 30, 1776, published a typical specimen entitled *The Pausing Loyal-ist:*

" To sign, or not to sign!—That is the question:
  Whether 't were better for an honest man
  To sign—and so be safe; or to resolve,
  Betide what will, against ' associations,'
  And, by retreating, shun them. To fly—I reck
  Not where—and, by that flight, t' escape
  Feathers and tar, and thousand other ills
  That Loyalty is heir to: 'tis a consummation
  Devoutly to be wished. To fly—to want—
  To want?—perchance to starve! Ay, there's the
     rub!
  For in that chance of want, what ills may come
  To patriot rage when I have left my all,
  Must give us pause! There's the respect
  That makes us trim, and bow to men we hate.
  For who would bear th' indignities o' the times,
  Congress decrees, and wild Convention plans,
  The laws controll'd, and inj'ries unredressed,
  The insolence of knaves, and thousand wrongs
  Which patient liegemen from vile rebels take,
  When he, sans doubt, might certain safety find
  Only by flying? Who would bend to fools
  And truckle thus to mad, mob-chosen upstarts,
  But that the dread of something after flight
  (In that blest country, where, yet, no moneyless

Poor wight can live) puzzles the will,
And makes ten thousands rather sign—and eat,
Than fly—to starve on Loyalty ! " . . .

There is a certain grim despair in the smiling condescension of such lines.

THE CONGRESS

Indeed it must have gone hard with these men who could trace their ancestry back to the days of the Normans to see themselves derided and perhaps persecuted by those whom they considered merely country laborers or town mechanics and shop-keepers. The Loyalist impression of the social standing of these fellows was pretty well summed up in the ballad, *The Congress,* written in 1776:

" These hardy knaves and stupid fools,
    Some apish and pragmatic mules,
    Some servile acquiescing tools,—
        These, these compose the Congress!

" When Jove resolved to send a curse,
    And all the woes of life rehearse,
    Not plague, not famine, but much worse—
        He cursed us with a Congress.

. . . .

110

"Good Lord! disperse this venal tribe;
 Their doctrine let no fools imbibe—
 Let Balaam no more asses ride,
     Nor burdens bear to Congress.

             .   .   .   .

"Old Catiline, and Cromwell too,
 Jack Cade, and his seditious crew,
 Hail brother-rebel at first view,
     And hope to meet the Congress."

This same sneering tone sounds through practically every poem of Tory origin. Caste is the hardest of all institutions to break down, and the fact was just as evident in the American Revolution as in any other great social upheaval. North and South the sneer was the same. A South Carolina Loyalist declared that

"Priests, tailors, and cobblers fill with heroes the
     camp,
 And sailors, like crawfish, crawl out of each
     swamp;"

while John Ferdinand Smyth, a New England Loyalist, in his ballad, *The Rebels,* similarly declared that

"With loud peals of laughter, your sides, sirs, would
     crack,

To see General Convict and Colonel Shoe-black,
With their hunting-shirts and rifle-guns;
See cobblers and quacks, rebel priests and the like,
Pettifoggers and barbers, with sword and with pike,
All strutting, the standard of Satan beside,
And honest names using, their black deeds to hide."

ON TOM PAINE

Nor were these sarcastic commentaries on the American warriors always general; they frequently dealt in personalities. The *New York Gazette* (August 11, 1779), the paper published by the James Rivington noted above, took delight in presenting numerous " personal tokens " similar to the following one on Tom Paine:

" Hail mighty Thomas! in whose works are seen
A mangled Morris and distorted Deane;
Whose splendid periods flash for Lee's defense,—
Replete with everything but Common Sense.
You, by whose labors no man e'er was wiser,
You, of invective great monopolizer;
O say, what name shall dignify the lays
Which now I consecrate to sing thy praise!
In pity tell by what exalted name
Thou would'st be damned to an eternal fame:
Shall Common Sense or Comus greet thine ear,
A piddling poet, or puffed pamphleteer?

· · · · · · · ·

By daily slanders earn thy daily food,
Exalt the wicked, and depress the good;
And having spent a lengthy life in evil,
Return again unto thy parent devil! "

In short, the Tory estimate of the enemy was nothing more or less than that expressed in the afore-mentioned *New York Gazette*, when *A Modern Catechism* (May 23, 1778) pronounced the instigators of the Revolution to be " an unprincipled and a disappointed faction in the mother country and an infernal, dark-designing group of men in America audaciously styling themselves a Congress, . . . obscure, pettifogging attorneys, bankrupt shop-keepers, outlawed smugglers, . . . wretched banditti, . . . the refuse and dregs of mankind." As the war progressed, however, the " dregs of mankind " became bolder and bolder in their sarcasm, while the blue-blooded satirists feared more and more to speak, until, as the day for the last scene at Yorktown approached, the Yankee humorists laughed alone and heard no mocking echo.

IV

YANKEE DOODLE

It is plain that of humorous verse, or, rather, humorous doggerel, there was no lack. It is very good proof of the abiding sense of humor in the American people that in those troubled and positively dangerous days they were able to see and enjoy the ludicrous side of the warfare. Not infrequently they seized upon the very satires of the enemy and hurled them back in his teeth. *Yankee Doodle*, for instance, has for itself just such a history. The tune of this popular ballad is older than most of the existing nations. In the twelfth century it was used as a chant in Catholic churches of Italy, and when played slowly doubtless served very well as a sacred air. But the melody was too easily learned to remain in such a limited service, and after 1200 we find it gradually working its way into the daily life of the ordinary peasant. It became a most popular vintage song in Spain and southern France; reached northward into Holland, where, as a reaper's song, it acquired the words " Yanker dudel, doodle down "; and at length entered England, where, before the reign of Charles I, it was a widely known nursery rhyme with the words:

> " Lucky Locket lost her pocket,
> Kitty Fisher found it—
> Nothing in it, nothing on it,
> But the binding round it."

In the days of the Puritan rule the Cavaliers wrote a song in ridicule of Cromwell, who, it is said, once rode into Oxford, mounted on a small Kentish horse and with his small plume tied into a knot:

> " Yankee doodle came to town
> Upon a Kentish pony;
> He stuck a feather in his cap
> And called him macaroni."

" Macaroni," it should be remembered, was a term frequently applied to London dudes.

Thus the song had served in many capacities when Dr. Richard Shuckburg, a surgeon in the

British army, seeing the raw New England rustics gazing in open-mouthed wonder at the English cannons and soldiers, suddenly conceived the idea of writing new words to the old tune to apply to the patriots. Many lines of the poem easily betray its origin:

" And there we see a thousand men,
    As rich as Squire David;
And what they wasted ev'ry day,
    I wish it could be saved.

    .   .   .   .   .

" And there I see a swamping gun,
    Large as a log of maple,
Upon a deuced little cart,
    A load for father's cattle.

" And every time they shoot it off,
    It takes a horn of powder,
And makes a noise like father's gun
    Only a nation louder.

" I went as nigh to one myself
    As 'Siah's underpinning;
And father went as nigh again,
    I thought the deuce was in him.

    .   .   .   .   .

116

" And there was Cap'n Washington,
    And gentlefolks about him;
    They say he's grown so 'tarnal proud
    He will not ride without 'em.

" He's got him on his meeting clothes,
    Upon a slapping stallion;
    He set the world along in rows,
    In hundreds and in millions."

But he laughs best who laughs last. The colonists liked the song, sang it as their own, and later, as they shot down the retreating British from behind walls and trees, they whistled it with such mocking vim that Cornwallis is said to have exclaimed, " I hope to God I shall never hear that damned tune again! "

Many a derisive ballad was composed by the rude bards of the camp and roared forth around the evening fire. Such a one was *The Battle of King's Mountain* (1781):

" 'Twas on a pleasant mountain
    The Tory heathen lay,—
    With a doughty major at their head,
    One Ferguson, they say.

Cornwallis had detached him,
A-thieving for to go,
And catch the Carolina men,
Or bring the rebels low."

. . . . . .

TAXATION OF AMERICA

As shown in previous paragraphs, these rude
camp-songs were accompanied by a continuous
stream of newspaper verse. Some of this we
have noted; room for one or two more specimens may perhaps be spared. It was in 1778
that a certain Peter St. John of Connecticut
wrote a long ballad entitled *Taxation of America*—a poem that pleased the colonists not only
by its ideas but by its swinging rhythm and a
refrain in the last line that gave it a devil-may-
care air quite irresistible:

" While I relate my story,
Americans give ear;
Of Britain's fading glory
You presently shall hear;
I'll give a true relation,
Attend to what I say
Concerning the taxation
Of North America.

" There are two mighty speakers,
   Who rule in Parliament,
Who ever have been seeking
   Some mischief to invent;
'Twas North and Bate, his father,
   The horrid plan did lay
A mighty tax to gather
   In North America.

" They searched the gloomy regions
   Of the infernal pit,
To find among their legions,
   One who excelled in wit;
To ask of him assistance,
   Or tell them how they may
Subdue without resistance
   This North America.

" Old Satan the arch-traitor,
   Who rules the burning lake,
Where his chief navigator
   Resolved a voyage to take;
For the Britannic ocean
   He launches far away,
To land he had no notion
   In North America.

" He takes his seat in Britain,
   It was his soul's intent
Great George's throne to sit on,
   And rule the Parliament;

His comrades were pursuing
A diabolic way,
For to complete the ruin,
Of North America.''

Thus the poet continued, doubtless to the great delight of the uncritical colonists and to the great disgust of the British *litterateurs* in the invading army.

FATE OF JOHN BURGOYNE

We have seen with what scorn the early failures of the English generals were received. As the war progressed and these leaders displayed no special brilliancy in the art of war, the scorn of the Yankees deepened, and a source of delight to all editors was poetry ridiculing these blundering soldiers. *The Fate of John Burgoyne* is a typical example:

'' When Jack, the king's commander,
Was going to his duty,
Through all the crowd he smiled and bowed
To every blooming beauty.

. . . .

'' To Hampton Court he first repairs
To kiss great George's hand, sirs;
Then to harangue on state affairs
Before he left the land, sirs.

120

" The ' Lower House ' sate mute as mouse
    To hear his great oration;
And ' all the peers,' with loudest cheers,
    Proclaimed him to the nation.

. . . .

" With great parade his march he made
    To gain his wished-for station,
While far and wide his minions hied
    To spread his ' Proclamation.'

. . . .

" But ah, the cruel fates of war!
    This boasted son of Britain,
When mounting his triumphal car,
    With sudden fear was smitten.

" The sons of freedom gathered round,
    His hostile bands confounded,
And when they'd fain have turned their back
    They found themselves surrounded!

" In vain they fought, in vain they fled;
    Their chief humane and tender,
To save the rest soon thought it best
    His forces to surrender." . . .

THE DANCE

All this must have been extremely amusing
to Burgoyne,—doubtless it " tickled " him
almost as much as another song of the day,

The Dance (1781), did Cornwallis,—that is if either one stopped long enough to read. However, the old saying declares that " he who runs may read," and according to this poem Cornwallis at least must have been a very fast reader.

" Cornwallis led a country dance,
 The like was never seen, sir,
  Much retrograde and much advance,
   And all with General Greene, sir.

" They rambled up and rambled down,
 Joined hands, then off they run, sir,
  Our General Greene to Charlestown,
   The earl to Wilmington, sir.

" Greene in the South then danced a set,
 And got a mighty name, sir,
  Cornwallis jigged with young Fayette,
   But suffered in his fame, sir.

 . . . .

" Quoth he, my guards are weary grown
 With footing country dances,
  They never at St. James's shone
   At capers, kicks or prances.

" Though men so gallant ne'er were seen,
 While sauntering on parade, sir,
  Or wriggling o'er the park's smooth green,
   Or at a masquerade, sir,

" Yet are red heels and long-laced skirts
    For stumps and briars meet, sir?
Or stand they chance with hunting shirts,
    Or hardy veteran feet, sir?

  .   .   .   .

" His music soon forgets to play—
    His feet can no more move, sir,
And all his bands now curse the day
    They jigged to our shore, sir.

" Now, Tories all, what can ye say?
    Come—is not this a griper,
That while your hopes are danced away,
    'Tis you must pay the piper? "

Many, many are the specimens which might
be presented; but will not these suffice to show
that those years of warfare were not such
dreary times after all? While the rough-
voiced regimentals shouted their rude ballads
through the tented streets, the friends at home
battered the enemy with a broad but none the
less effective satire. The effect of a taunt on
a discouraged foe is not to be belittled, and, for
aught we know, the scornful jokes of the
colonial wits may have done a part in putting
the red-coats to flight not yet sufficiently recognized in our histories of the momentous period.

V

As has been intimated, much of the Revolutionary wit and humor was anonymous; here and there, however, among the musty newspapers and rudely printed pamphlets we meet with a familiar name. On the Tory side the leaders in the merry battle were undoubtedly Jonathan Odell and Joseph Stansbury, while the champions of satire for the patriots were just as undoubtedly Francis Hopkinson, Philip Freneau, and the popular member of the sarcastic group known as the "Hartford Wits," John Trumbull. At times these men gave Laughter good cause for "holding both his sides," while their particular victim of the moment must doubtless have felt, as Artemus Ward said Jefferson Davis did, that "it would have been worth ten dollars in his pocket if he had never been born." For in those early days men spared not one another; they hit hard and

THE HUMOR OF THE REVOLUTION

no sense of refinement withheld them from bitter and even vulgar personalities.

It would have been difficult to find two men more unlike in their natures than the two Loyalists, Jonathan Odell, the fiery, and Joseph Stansbury, the gentle. Both loved England with a jealous love; but the one hated her enemies forever, the other forgave them freely. Odell thundered with a malignant scowl; Stansbury sang with an amused smile.

JONATHAN ODELL

The first of these, Jonathan Odell, was born at Newark, New Jersey, in 1737. His ancestors had been in America for more than one hundred years; according to our view, therefore, he should have had better taste than to be a Tory. After graduating from the College of New Jersey (Princeton) in 1754, he studied medicine, became a surgeon in the British army, and for some time served in the West Indies. At length he came to the conclusion that it was more important to improve men's souls than to cure their bodies, and, consequently, in 1767, he became rector of St. Mary's parish at Burlington, New Jersey. He was

125

always a zealous worker in any movement that gained his sympathy, and he soon had the reputation of being a godly and fearless man.

Like his fellow Tory, Stansbury, he was with the colonists in their efforts to have oppressive measures repealed; but, as a preacher and as a Loyalist, he was opposed to violence,—especially violence toward England. Yet, up to the time of the Battle of Bunker Hill he took no part in the hot debates of the day. He had his opinions, nevertheless, vigorous, stubborn opinions too, and they soon got him into trouble. In October, 1775, two letters of his were opened by suspicious committeemen, and certain Tory expressions in these missives caused his arrest. Boldly he declared his neutrality. "I presumed it reasonable in me," he said in after years, "to expect I should be indulged in the unmolested enjoyment of my private sentiments so long as I did not attempt to influence the sentiments or conduct of other men."

But Odell did not long live up to this theory. June 4, 1776, was King George's birthday. The loyal preacher wrote a song on the happy occasion, and a number of British captives in the neighborhood, meeting for a banquet on an island in the Delaware River, roared forth with great enthusiasm this poetical tribute to their ruler. On July 20 Odell was adjudged a dangerous person and was immediately compelled to sign a pledge that he would remain "within a circle of eight miles from the court house of the city of Burlington." In December, 1776, the town was shelled to keep the Hessians away, and Odell very prudently fled, hid for some time in the home of a Quakeress, and at length escaped to New York City, where he received a warm welcome. An experienced soldier, a physician, a clergyman, a scholar, a wit, and a good fellow besides, he was heartily received in every circle of the city's social life. But not a word of satire yet. Three years passed,—three years of valuable service to the British; but even then he refused to say to the patriot: "Thou fool."

In the preface, however, to one of the satires which finally did burst from him, he expressed this sentiment: "The masters of reason have decided that when doctrines and practices have been fairly examined and proved to be contrary to truth and injurious to society, then and not before may ridicule be lawfully employed in the service of virtue." The doctrines and practices of the patriots had now been fairly exam-

127

ined; he could stand the strain no longer; his time for a deliverance had come. In September, 1779, he opened up his batteries. The first shot was *The Word of Congress;* in November came the second and the third, *The Congratulation* and *The Feu de Joi,* and in December the fourth and last, *The American Times.*

No gentleness here. Hot wrath rings through them all. Bitter scorn—too bitter for hearty laughter—poisons their every line. They remind one of Pope's keen thrusts; and indeed they are largely modelled after that satirist's masterpieces. The people, Odell declares, have been poisoned by a deceptive drink, a cup filled with so-called liberty. And who made this drink?

" What group of wizards next salutes my eyes—
United comrades, quadruple allies?
Bostonian Cooper, with his Hancock joined,
Adams with Adams, one in heart and mind.
Sprung from the soil where witches swarmed of
    yore,
They come well skilled in necromantic lore;
    .   .   .   .
See! the smoke rises from the cursed drench,
And poisons all the air with horrid stench.

128

" Celestial muse, I fear 'twill make thee hot
To count the vile ingredients of the pot;
Dire incantations, words of death, they mix
With noxious plants, and water from the Styx;
Treason's rank flowers, Ambition's swelling fruits,
Hypocrisy in seeds, and Fraud in roots,
Bundles of Lies fresh gathered in their prime,
And stalks of Calumny grown stale with time;
Handfuls of Zeal's intoxicating leaves,
Riot in bunches, Cruelty in sheaves,
Slices of Cunning cut exceeding thin,
Kernels of Malice, rotten core of Sin,
Branches of Persecutors, boughs of Thrall,
And sprigs of Persecution, dipt in Gall." . . .

Democracy! How the word nauseates him!
A foul being, he declares, and a dangerous
one,—a wolf in sheep's clothing. What names
shall he apply to the creature? " Bless me! "
he exclaims in *The American Times,*

" Bless me! what formidable figure's this
That interrupts my words with saucy hiss?
She seems at least a woman by her face,
With harlot smiles adorned and winning grace.
A glittering gorget on her breast she wears;
The shining silver two inscriptions bears:
' Servant of Servants,' in a laurel wreath,
But ' Lord of Lords ' is written underneath.

    .   .   .   .

This is Democracy—the case is plain;
She comes attended by a motley train;
Addresses to the people some unfold;
Rods, scourges, fetters, axes, others hold;
The sorceress waves her magic wand about,
And models at her will the rabble rout;
Here Violence puts on a close disguise,
And Public Spirit's character belies.
The dress of Policy see Cunning steal,
And Persecution wear the coat of Zeal;
Hypocrisy Religion's garb assume,
Fraud Virtue strip, and figure in her room;
With other changes tedious to relate,
All emblematic of our present state.''

We might fill a volume with the pretty
things that have been said about Democracy.
We might quote from Thomas Jefferson to
Thomas Watson, and when we were through we
might well conclude that '' the greatest thing
in the world'' is not Love, but—Democracy.
But, shouts Odell, see the results of Democracy!
The plebians have arisen; the world is turned
upside down.

'' From the back woods half savages came down,
And awkward troops paraded every town.
Committees and conventions met by scores;

Justice was banished, Law turned out of doors;
Disorder seemed to overset the land;
They who appeared to rule, the tumult fanned.''

And behold the statesmenship of the new *regime!* How self-possessed! What dignity! What state-craft!

'' There Folly runs with eagerness about,
And prompts the cheated populace to shout;
Here paper-dollars meagre Famine holds,
There votes of Congress Tyranny unfolds;

. . . .

Confusion blows her trump—and far and wide
The noise is heard—the plough is laid aside;
The awl, the needle, and the shuttle drops;
Tools change to swords, and camps succeed to shops;

. . . .

From garrets, cellars, rushing through the street,
The new-born statesmen in committees meet;
Legions of senators infest the land,
And mushroom generals thick as mushrooms stand.''

By this time we evidently have grasped the idea that Odell was dreadfully in earnest. His Tory heart must have been sadly wrung at times. No chance for improvement, he declares; the case is quite hopeless. Why, the very soil sprouts fools; *i. e.,* patriots.

131

" Was Samuel Adams to become a ghost,
Another Adams would assume his post;
Was bustling Hancock numbered with the dead,
Another full as wise might raise his head.

. . . .

Or what if Washington should close his scene,
Could none succeed him?—Is there not a Greene?
Knave after knave as easy we could join,
As new emissions of the paper coin.
When it became the high United States
To send their envoys to Versailles' proud gates,
Were not three ministers produced at once?
Delicious group, fanatic, deist, dunce!
And what if Lee, and what if Silas fell,
Or what if Franklin should go down to hell,
Why should we grieve?—the land 'tis understood
Can furnish hundreds equally as good."

Do not forget for a moment that our scornful friend was a clergyman—so conscientious a clergyman, in fact, that he could not see how any self-respecting parson could preach to such miserable creatures as the patriots. Evidently he had forgotten the " lost sheep " doctrine of Christianity. Now, one of the fieriest patriotic preachers of the day was George Duffield, for some time chaplain of the Continental Congress. Odell was heartily ashamed of the fellow; he said so in unmistakable terms:

" A saint of old, as learned monks have said,
  Preached to the fish—the fish his voice obeyed,
  The same good man convened the grunting herd—
  Who bowed obedient to his pow'rful word.
  Such energy has truth in days of yore;
  Falsehood and nonsense, in our days, have more.
  Duffield avows them to be all in all,
  And mounts or quits the pulpit, at their call.

  .   .   .   .

  Chaplain of Congress give him to become,
  Light may be dark, and oracles be dumb,
  It pleased Saint Anthony to preach to brutes—
  To preach to devils best with Duffield suits! "

Vanity, vanity, saith the preacher; all in vanity. Thus Odell gazed with disgust upon the originators of all this confusion. He espied the smirking, splotched face of Tom Paine, and the parson's fury descended upon that bitter enemy of all parsons. See, exclaimed Odell, how the miscreants work together!

" Others apart in some obscure recess,
  The studied lie for publication dress:
  Prepare the vague report, fallacious tale.
  Invent fresh calumnies, revive the stale,
  Pervert all records sacred and profane,—
  And chief among them stands the villain Paine.
  This scribbling imp, 'tis said, from London came,
  That seat of glory intermixed with shame.

  .   .   .   .

What cannot ceaseless impudence produce?
Old Franklin knows its value, and its use:
He caught at Paine, relieved his wretched plight,
And gave him notes, and set him down to write.
Fire from the Doctor's hints the miscreant took,
Discarded truth, and soon produced a book,—
A pamphlet which, without the least pretence
To reason, bore the name of ' Common Sense.'

.   .   .   .

Sense, reason, judgment were abashed and fled,
And Congress reigned triumphant in their stead."

At this distant day we look back upon
George Washington as almost a god. We perhaps forget that the scorn of the blue-bloods
and the sarcasm of the town wits once burnt
into his soul and at times severely shook his
self-possession. Washington was a very " human " being of the eighteenth century, and
jokers doubtless had the laugh on him just as
frequently as on any other personage of the
day. Odell himself left his gloves at home
when he began to handle the General. Now,
cried he,

" Strike up, hell's music! roar, infernal drums!
Discharge the cannon! Lo, the warrior comes!
He comes, not tame as on Ohio's banks,

But rampant at the head of ragged ranks.
Hunger and itch are with him—Gates and Wayne!
And all the lice of Egypt in his train.

   .   .   .   .

Hear thy indictment, Washington, at large;
Attend and listen to the solemn charge:
Thou hast supported an atrocious cause
Against thy king, thy country, and the laws;
Committed perjury, encouraged lies,
Forced conscience, broken the most sacred ties;
Myriads of wives and fathers at thy hand
Their slaughtered husbands, slaughtered sons, de-
    mand;

   .   .   .   .

Innumerable crimes on thee must fall—
For thou maintainest, thou defendest all.

   .   .   .   .

Go, wretched author of thy country's grief,
Patron of villainy, of villains chief;
Seek with thy cursed crew the central gloom,
Ere Truth's avenging sword begin thy doom."

Would that we might linger over more of
Odell's taunting words. The objects of his sarcasm have long since gone to their reward and
would not mind the further repetition of his
lines. My readers might, however;—and men
fear the living rather than the dead. All that
has been said simply goes to show that times

were not monotonous in the days of the Revolution, and that people laughed now and then in spite of Bunker Hill and Valley Forge. Odell's compliments were purposely spread far and wide by the Tory element, and all were of that sweet flavor found above in his views of Tom Paine or George Washington or of that particular enemy of his, General Charles Lee.

" Arise, ye Fiends, from dark Cocytus' brink;
  Soot all my paper, sulphurize my ink;
  So with my theme the colors shall agree,
  Brimstone and black—the livery of Lee."

Such lines, however, must have added to the laughter of the patriots as well as of the Loyalists; for the former, with the tide of battle in their favor, could well afford to enjoy the vexation of the enemy.

Like some old Confederate soldiers, Odell was never " reconstructed." Even after he had fled to Nova Scotia and was leading a prosperous life there he never missed an opportunity to curse the Americans roundly, and to his dying day he always had some pet scheme up his sleeve by which he hoped to down the Yankees and make the United States a Paradise for Loyalists.

VI

" Though ruined so deeply no angel can save,
   The empire dismembered, our king made a slave,
   Still loving, revering, we shout forth honestly—
        God save the king!
   Though fated to banishment, poverty, death,
   Our hearts are unaltered, and with our last breath
   Loyal to George, we'll pray most fervently—
        Glory and joy crown the king! "

Thus, after the Tories had lost their all, the other leader of their wits, Joseph Stansbury, sang cheerily. Gentle, reasonable, forgiving, he was a more lovable though less effective man than his friend Odell. He was born in London in 1740; was educated at St. Paul's School, where he showed a talent for literature; and came to America in 1769. He soon entered business life at Philadelphia, and, because of his social qualities, especially his ability to compose and sing songs for all sorts of ceremonies, he speedily became a welcomed member of every circle in the city.

He saw with keen regret the tyrannical
methods pursued by his native country and his
earlier poems show him to have been in sympathy with the colonial strugglers. He could
not see, however, that separation and independence were the proper remedies for the distress;
consequently in 1775 and 1776 we find him
classed among the hated Tories. Nevertheless, during the latter year and 1777 he continued his business in the city, where, during
the British occupation, he was of course exceedingly popular. But in 1778 he deemed it
wise to withdraw and remain with the British
troops in New York City. After the surrender
he removed to a New Jersey village, but even
there he found no peace; for, as a Loyalist, he
was soon cast into prison at Burlington. Upon
his promising to leave the State within nine
days, he was allowed to remove in August,
1783, to Nova Scotia, where in lonely exile he
remained until the autumn of 1785. The separation from his wife and children became un-
bearable; he returned to Philadelphia; he had
scarcely entered his home when a letter tossed
through a window, warned him to flee; and
once more he was a forlorn wanderer. In

1793, however, he found a home among the more liberal people of New York City, and there he died in 1809.

Such was the unforgiving bitterness of the Revolutionary times. At this late day we can see that this gentle Loyalist did not deserve the harsh treatment accorded him. Even his wittiest verses have little of animosity; they are more of smiles than of sneers. Until 1776 he said scarcely one satirical word about the patriots; for it was his hope that war could be averted. But one hot day in that year an incident so attacked his risibility that he could no longer stand the strain; and the poetry came. A certain colonial parson, William Piercy, was preaching a fiery sermon to the Philadelphia militia, and had placed behind himself a hideously ugly negro, who with unabating zeal fanned the speaker. The next morning a stanza by Stansbury was flying through the streets:

" To preach up, friend Piercy, at this critical season
    Resistance to Britain is not very civil,
Yet what can we look for but faction and treason,
    From a flaming enthusiast—fanned by the
        devil? ''

From this time forth Stansbury was frequently called upon by the Loyalists for songs on this or that occasion. Fortunately for himself but unfortunately for us, he burnt a great mass of his papers immediately after the surrender; but from what remains we can surmise that he must have caused many a roar of laughter in the old days of Tory festivity. The year 1780, however, was not one of joy for British sympathizers. That very year the patriots grew so bold as to rush within the borders of New York City, steal a quantity of hay, and set several houses on fire. Stansbury, disgusted with the procrastination of the British leader, Sir Henry Clinton, turned his sarcasm upon this amusement-loving soldier,—one form of amusement which Clinton is said not to have relished:

> " ' Has the Marquis La Fayette
> Taken off all our hay yet? '
> Says Clinton to the wise heads around him:
> ' Yes, faith, Sir Harry,
> Each stack he did carry,
> And likewise the cattle—confound him!
>
> " ' Besides, he now goes,
> Just under your nose,
> To burn all the houses to cinder! '

' If that be his project,
It is not an object
Worth a great man's attempting to hinder.

" ' For forage and house
I care not a louse;
For revenge, let the Loyalists bellow;
I swear I'll not do more
To keep them in humor,
Than play on my violoncello.

" ' If growlers complain,
I inactive remain—
Will do nothing, nor let any others!
'Tis sure no new thing
To serve thus our king—
Witness Burgoyne, and two famous Brothers!' "

Stansbury, like his comrade, Odell, was not easily discouraged. Even when Cornwallis surrendered, the witty Loyalist made sturdy efforts to be optimistic. In that gloomy day he wrote for the edification of the frightened Tories of New York City a few stanzas of encouragement:

" I've heard in old times that a sage used to say,
The seasons were nothing, December or May;
The heat or the cold never entered his plan—
That all should be happy whenever they can.

.   .   .   .

" He happened to enter this world the same day
With the supple, complying, famed Vicar of Bray:
Through both of their lives the same principle ran—
My boys, we'll be happy as long as we can.

" Time-serving I hate, yet I see no good reason
A leaf from their book shall be thought out of sea-
son:
When kicked like a football from Sheba to Dan—
Egad, let's be happy as long as we can. . . ."

Before, however, there was ever any necessity for such a song of encouragement, while
yet the British were enjoying the hospitality of
New York City, and every Tory foresaw an
early and an easy victory, Stansbury furnished
many a pleasant line for his friends,—lines
more enjoyable perhaps because lacking all the
bitterness of those by the other satirist, Odell.
Those were gay houses in the city, and Stansbury's convivial poems added much to the
gaiety. In 1781, for example, he wrote for a
" venison dinner at Mr. Bunyan's " a rollicking
song containing such verses as

" But through near our lines they're too cautious to
tarry,
What courage they shew when a hen-roost they
harry!

Who can wonder that poultry and oxen and swine
Seek shelter in York from such valor divine,—
While Washington's jaws and the Frenchman's are
    aching
The spoil they have lost, to be boiling and baking.

" Let Clinton and Arnold bring both to subjection,
And send us more geese here to seek our protection.
Their flesh and their feathers shall meet a kind
    greeting;
A fat rebel turkey is excellent eating,
A lamb fat as butter and white as a chicken—
These sorts of tame rebels are excellent pickin'.

" To-day a wild rebel has smoked on the table;
You've cut him and sliced him as long as you're
    able.
He bounded like Congo,* and bade you defiance,
And placed on his running his greatest reliance;
But fate overtook him and brought him before ye,
To shew how rebellion will wind up her story. . . ."

It has often been said that the chief difference between a revolution and a rebellion is that
the one succeeds and the other does not. Just
there is where Stansbury and Odell and we dis-
agreed. They looked upon us as rebels; we

---

*Congo was a Tory nickname for the Continental Congress.

considered ourselves revolutionists. War decided that we were the latter, and Stansbury quietly acquiesced,—while the violent Odell never could accept the decision. It was the gentler Loyalist, exiled as he was from family and home, who wrote the lines that should have gone to the heart of Tory and patriot alike:

" Now this war at length is o'er,
Let us think of it no more;
Every party lie or name,
Cancel as our mutual shame;
Bid each wound of faction close—
Blushing we were ever foes."

VII

Of course, for a time, the Tories considered the American Revolution a huge joke. Not so to many of the colonial fathers. Indeed, some fun-makers were sorely needed by several of those solemn-faced founders of our nation. To them life was a little too earnest; they took themselves perhaps a trifle too seriously. Only a few of these greater men dared to risk their reputation for solidness by joking *openly* whenever they felt like it; and naturally these choice spirits stand out conspicuously because of their very loneliness. Among the common folk there was, of course, much rough humor and satire; but we speak now of the moulders of the Commonwealth. Of those conspicuous for their audacity in being funny in public one of the most daring in his defiance toward the ancient idea that all great people must be solemn was Francis Hopkinson.

FRANCIS HOPKINSON

John Adams, in a letter to Mrs. Adams, speaks of him as "a painter and a poet." "He is," continues that grave statesman, "one of your pretty, little, curious, ingenious gentlemen. . . . His head is not bigger than a large apple." Yet, even Adams, who was amused to see such a specimen of dainty manhood, confessed that he was a gentleman of merit. And Hopkinson was more than that. Says Moses Coit Tyler, in his *Literary History of the American Revolution:* "He was a distinguished practitioner of the law; he became an eminent judge; he was a statesman trained by much study and experience; he was a mathematician, a chemist, a physicist, a mechanician, an inventor, a musician, and a composer of music, a man of literary knowledge and practice, a writer of airy and dainty songs, a clever artist with pencil and brush, and a humorist of unmistakable power." And with it all was a kindness of heart that made him a friend of every creature—even a Tory! The timid doves waited for him daily in his yard, and, as he approached them, flew to meet him, and perched

146

upon his shoulders and head. A little mouse came regularly at meal time and played unafrighted about his feet. All men loved him—all except the Tories and the British, and of course they didn't count, in his estimation.

Born in Philadelphia in 1737, Hopkinson was left an orphan at the age of fourteen. He was educated at the College of Philadelphia, afterwards the University of Pennsylvania, and was a member of the first graduating class in 1757. Three years later he received the degree of Master of Arts. In 1761 he was admitted to the bar, and very soon gained a reputation for high legal ability. That at this early date he had gained the confidence of the leading officials is evidenced by the fact that in the same year, 1761, he was chosen secretary of the conference between Pennsylvania and the Indians,—a conference, by the way, which gave him the idea for his once famous poem, *The Treaty*. In 1766 he went to England, remained fourteen months, and returned with an amount of information and culture that proved he had kept his eyes exceedingly wide open. Some of the great men of the day evidently thought so too; for in 1772, on the recommendation of

Lord North, he was appointed collector of customs at Newcastle, New Jersey, and in 1774 was made a member of the council of that colony. In the meantime he had married a granddaughter of the founder of Bordentown, New Jersey, and of course henceforth his main interests were in that little commonwealth.

After all the favors he had received from the British government, he might well have been expected to become a Tory. But he loved America better than position, and from the moment that serious trouble began to brew, he was always present at the brewing. In 1776 he was the representative of New Jersey in the Continental Congress, was a signer of the Declaration of Independence, served on numerous committees, and was ever wielding a most facile pen (or quill, shall we say?) in behalf of the new nation; while among the literary works of his busy brain in those heated days were *The Pretty Story* (1774), *The Prophecy* (1776), *The Political Catechism* (1777), and a host of sharp letters, sarcastic essays, and satirical poems.

His reward came with the success of the colonies. From 1779 until 1789 he was judge of the admiralty for Pennsylvania, was appointed United States district judge for the same State in 1790, and was ever considered by the greatest officials a man worthy of consultation and attention. Full of years and honor, he died in Philadelphia in 1791. Shortly after his death, his works were issued under the title, *The Miscellaneous Essays and Occasional Writings of Francis Hopkinson.*

The average reader of to-day knows Francis Hopkinson through one piece, *The Battle of the Kegs.* And, if he had written nothing else, he is worthy of remembrance for that sly bit of sarcasm. Undoubtedly it was the most popular ballad written in Revolutionary days. It was copied in every colony; it was recited at social functions; and public speakers, when wishing to have the laugh on the British, quoted stanzas from it. The incident which caused the poem was laughable in itself, and Hopkinson measured up to his opportunity. Kegs charged with powder were floated down the river to destroy the British fleet lying before Philadelphia, with the result that the English soldiers spent the day bravely *shooting kegs!* It must have been galling to Tories to read in New York and Philadelphia and Boston papers such lines as these:

" Gallants attend and hear a friend
　　Trill forth harmonious ditty,
　Strange things I'll tell which late befell
　　In Philadelphia city.

" 'Twas early day, as poets say,
　　Just when the sun was rising,
　A soldier stood on a log of wood
　　And saw a thing surprising.

" As in amaze he stood to gaze,
　　The truth can't be denied, sir,
　He spied a score of kegs or more
　　Come floating down the tide, sir.

　　·　　·　　·　　·　　·　　·

" Now up and down throughout the town,
　　Most frantic scenes were acted;
　And some ran here and others there,
　　Like men almost distracted.

　　·　　·　　·　　·　　·

" ' Arise ! Arise ! ' Sir Erskine cries,
　　' The rebels—more's the pity,
　Without a boat are all afloat,
　　And ranged before the city.

" ' The motley crew, in vessels new,
　　With Satan for their guide, sir,
　Packed up in bags or wooden kegs,
　　Come driving down the tide, sir.

150

" ' Therefore prepare for bloody war,
    These kegs must all be routed,
Or surely we despised shall be,
    And British courage doubted.'

" The royal band now ready stand
    All ranged in dread array, sir,
With stomach stout to see it out,
    And make a bloody day, sir.

" The cannons roar from shore to shore,
    The small arms make a rattle;
Since war began I'm sure no man
    E'er saw so strange a battle.

.   .   .   .

" The fish below swam to and fro,
    Attacked from every quarter;
Why sure, thought they, the devil's to pay
    'Mongst folks above the water!

" The kegs, 'tis said, though strongly made,
    Of rebel staves and hoops, sir,
Could not oppose their powerful foes,
    The conquering British troops, sir.

.   .   .   .

" A hundred men with each a pen,
    Or more upon my word, sir,
It is most true would be too few,
    Their valor to record, sir.

"Such feats did they perform that day
  Against those wicked kegs, sir,
That years to come if they get home,
  They'll make their boasts and brags, sir!"

Is it not plain that there is really no bitterness here? It is characteristic of Hopkinson. Always more amused than angered, he simply had a good-humored laugh over the follies of his opponents. Evidently he kept in mind the words of his contemporary Robert Burns—

"O wad some Pow'r the giftie gie us
  To see oursels as others see us!"—

and did his utmost to help the Tories and British in their efforts along this line. Yet, it was not lack of serious principle that caused him to assume this good-natured levity. There were times when Hopkinson did not mince words. Hear his expressions in a letter to Joseph Galloway, a man who had proved himself a hypocrite:

"Now that you have gained the summit of your ambitious hopes, the reward of your forfeited honor, that dear-bought gratification, to obtain which you have given your name to infamy and your soul to per-

152

dition—now that you sit in Philadelphia, the nominal governor of Pennsylvania, give me leave to address a few words of truth to your corrupted heart. Retire for a moment from the avocations and honors of your new superintendency, and review the steps by which you have mounted the stage of power—steps reeking with the blood of your innocent country.

" When the storm was gathering dark and dreary over this devoted country, when America stood in need of all the exertions which her best patriots and most confidential citizens could make, you stepped forward—you offered yourself a candidate, and, with unwearied diligence, solicited a seat in the American Congress. Your seeming sincerity and your loud complaints against the unjust usurpations of the British legislature gained the confidence of your country. You were elected; you took your seat in Congress—and let posterity remember that while you were vehemently declaiming in that venerable senate against British tyranny, and with hypocritical zeal urging a noble stand in behalf of the liberties of your country, you were at the same time betraying their secrets, ridiculing their economy, and making sport of their conduct. . . .

" The temporary reward of iniquity you now hold will soon shirk from your grasp. . . . This you know, and the reflection must even now throw a gloom of horror over your enjoyments, which the glittering tinsel of your new superintendency cannot illumine. Look back, and all is guilt—look forward, and all is dread! When the history of the present time shall be recorded, the names of Galloway and Cunningham will not be omitted; and posterity will wonder at the extreme obduracy of which the human heart is capable, and at the unmeasurable difference between a traitor and a Washington."

If further proof were needed that this dainty-looking, art-loving gentleman could on occasion wield a sarcastic pen dipped in fluid bitterness, we might well turn to his *Letter Written by a Foreigner on His Travels,* in which he causes his " foreigner " to say concerning England:

" The extreme ignorance of the common people of this civilized country can scarce be credited. In general they know nothing beyond the particular branch of business which their parents or the parish happened to choose for them. This, indeed, they practise with unremitting diligence, but never think of extending their knowledge farther.

" A manufacturer has been brought up a maker of pin-heads. He has been at this business forty years and, of course, makes pin-heads with great dexterity; but he cannot make a whole pin to save his life. He thinks it is the perfection of human nature to make pin-heads. He leaves other matters to inferior abilities. It is enough for him that he believes in the Athanasian Creed, reverences the splendor of the court, and makes pin-heads. This he conceives to be the sum-total of religion, politics, and trade. He is sure that London is the finest city in the world; Black-friars Bridge the most superb of all possible bridges; and the river Thames the largest river in the universe. It is in vain to tell him that there are many rivers in America, in comparison of which the Thames is but a ditch; that there are single provinces there larger than all England; and that the colonies . . . are vastly more extensive than England, Wales, Scotland and Ireland, taken all together—he cannot conceive this. He goes into his best parlor, and looks on a map of England, four feet square; on the other side of the room he sees a map of North and South America, not more than two feet square, and exclaims: ' How can these things be! It is altogether impossible!' . . . Talk to him of the British constitution, he will tell you it is a glorious constitution; ask him what it is, and he is ignorant of its first principles; but he is sure that he can make and sell pin-heads under it. . . ."

This, however, was not the usual Francis Hopkinson. He preferred not to hiss, but to laugh his opponent out of court. If ever you enter one of the greater libraries of our country, ask for his *Pretty Story* (printed the very day the first Continental Congress met), and enjoy some very gentle yet very real humor.

155

You will find it to be a lively little allegory
telling the story of the disturbance between
the mother country and the colonies down to the
year 1774. England is represented by the Old
Farm, America by the New, while the Nobleman is the King, and his Wife is Parliament.
A few bits from it, to show its flavor:

" Once upon a time, a great while ago, there lived
a certain Nobleman, who had long possessed a very
valuable Farm, and had a great number of children
and grand-children. Besides the annual profits of his
land, which were very considerable, he kept a large
shop of goods; and being very successful in trade, he
became, in process of time, exceeding rich and powerful, insomuch that all his neighbors feared and re-
spected him. . . . Now, it came to pass that this Nobleman had, by some means or other, obtained a right
to an immense tract of wild uncultivated country at
a vast distance from his mansion house. But he set
little store by this acquisition, as it yielded him no
profit; nor was it likely to do so, being not only difficult of access on account of the distance, but was also
overrun with innumerable wild beasts very fierce and
savage,—so that it would be extremely dangerous to
attempt taking possession of it.

" In process of time, however, some of his children,
more stout and enterprising than the rest, requested
leave of their Father to go and settle on this distant

156

tract of land." [Then follows a list of the rules laid down by the king for the conduct of the settlers and the promises made by him. The new land showed prospects of becoming an earthly Paradise; but at length troubles began to come, as in every Paradise. The Nobleman's Wife began to cast envious looks towards the new home, and after a time issued an edict] " setting forth that whereas the tailors of her family were greatly injured by the people of the New Farm, inasmuch as they presumed to make their own clothes, whereby the said tailors were deprived of the benefit of their custom, it was therefore ordained that for the future the new settlers should not be permitted to have amongst them any shears or scissors larger than a certain fixed size. In consequence of this, our adventurers were compelled to have their clothes made by their Father's tailors; but out of regard to the old Gentleman, they patiently submitted to this grievance. . . . She [the Wife] persuaded her Husband to send amongst them, from time to time, a number of the most lazy and useless of her servants, under the specious pretext of defending them in their settlements and of assisting to destroy the wild beasts, but in fact, to rid his own house of their company, not having employment for them, and at the same time to be a watch and a check upon the people of the New Farm."

The story then declares that the Nobleman's Steward had debauched the Nobleman's Wife and had persuaded her to wear two padlocks on her lips so that when he opened one she could cry only " No," and when the other, only " Yes." The Steward then persuaded the Nobleman, who was now in his dotage, to place a heavy tax on several articles to be bought only at his shop, notably Water-Gruel [tea]. But the settlers would have none of it, and allowed the gruel to sour by the roadside. And " one of the new settlers, whose name was Jack [Boston], either from a keener sense of the injuries attempted against him, or from the necessity of his situation, which was such that he could not send back the Gruel because of a number of mercenaries whom his Father had stationed before his house to watch and be a check upon his conduct,—he, I say, being almost driven to despair, fell to work and with great zeal stove to pieces the casks of Gruel which had been sent him and utterly demolished the whole cargo. . . . The old Gentleman fell into great wrath, declaring that his absent children meant to throw off all dependence upon him, and to become altogether disobedient. His Wife also tore the padlocks from her lips, and raved and stormed like a Billingsgate. The

Steward lost all patience and moderation, swearing most profanely that he would leave no stone unturned until he had humbled the settlers of the New Farm at his feet, and caused their Father to trample on their necks. Moreover, the Gruel Merchants roared and bellowed for the loss of their Gruel; and the clerks and apprentices were in the utmost consternation lest the people of the New Farm should again agree to have no dealings with their Father's shop." Immediately an immense padlock was fastened upon Jack's gate, and an overseer was sent to Jack's home to " break his spirit."

Jack appealed to his neighbors for supplies, and " seasonable bounty was handed to Jack over the garden wall, all access to the front of his house being shut up." Moreover, Jack's Family held consultations about the matter; but the Overseer " wrote a thundering prohibition, much like a Pope's Bull, which he caused to be pasted up in every room in the house; in which he declared and protested that these meetings were treasonable, traitorous, and rebellious, contrary to the dignity of their Father and inconsistent with the omnipotence of their Mother-in-Law; denouncing also terrible punishments against any two of the Family who should from thenceforth be seen whispering together, and strictly forbidding the domestics to hold any more meetings in the garret or stable.

" These harsh and unconstitutional proceedings irritated Jack and the other inhabitants of the New Farm to such a degree that . . .

Caetera desunt "

Hopkinson refuses to prophesy what will happen; he leaves it to the gentlemen who were just then assembling in the hall of Congress not far from the book-stall where the *Pretty Story* was being exhibited.

If you will look into the story for yourself, you will see how well sustained, how interesting at all points, how full of bright surprises the genial narrative is. There is a flavor of French vivacity and French simplicity about it that charms one. We should not be surprised, therefore, to find that this man wrote some of the daintiest lyrics of early days—in some instances, exquisite little things that might well be revived and made popular through musical setting.

But the times were rather adverse toward love-lyrics and nature poems, and Hopkinson's talent was turned to the more immediately useful field of satirical verse. There were during those dangerous days, undoubtedly, numerous fickle creatures—'' the summer soldier and the sunshine patriot,'' as Tom Paine's *Crisis* called them—men who were valiant patriots when the Americans held the city and zealous Tories when the British came to town; and just such a sharp pen as Hopkinson's was needed for such people. The neat fable, *The Birds, the Beasts, and the Bat,* leaves no doubt as to his opinion of such turn-coats.

> '' A war broke out in former days—
>   If all is true that Æsop says—
>   Between the birds that haunt the grove
>   And beasts that wild in forests rove.
>
>   .   .   .   .
>
>   From every tribe vast numbers came
>   To fight for freedom, as for fame.
>
>   .   .   .   .
>
>   The bat—half bird, half beast—was there,
>   Nor would for *this* or *that* declare,—
>   Waiting till conquest should decide
>   Which was the strongest, safest side.
>
>   .   .   .   .

161

The birds in fierce assault, 'tis said,
Amongst the foe such havoc made—
That, panic-struck, the beasts retreat
Amazed, and victory seemed complete.
The observant bat, with squeaking tone,
Cried, ' Bravo, Birds! The day's our own;
For now I am proud to claim a place
Amongst your bold aspiring race.'

. . . .

" But now the beasts, ashamed of flight,
With rallied force renew the fight;

. . . .

Enraged, advance—push on the fray
And claim the honors of the day.
The bat, still hovering to and fro,
Observed how things were like to go.

. . . .

' Push on,' quoth he, ' Our's is the day!
We'll chase these rebel birds away,
And reign supreme—for who but we
Of earth and air the lords should be? '

. . . .

" Now in their turn the beasts must yield
The bloody laurels of the field.

. . . .

" Once more the bat with courtly voice,
' Hail, noble birds! Much I rejoice
In your success and come to claim
My share of conquest and of fame.'

The birds the faithless wretch despise:
' Hence, traitor, hence! ' the eagle cries;
' No more, as you just vengeance fear,
Amongst our honored ranks appear.'
The bat, disowned, in some old shed
Now seeks to hide his exiled head;
Nor dares his leathern wings display
From rising morn to setting day."

. . . .

It was true. Many a Tory, in the end, felt
inclined " in some old shed . . . to hide his
exiled head." And to good-natured Hopkinson their futile efforts to destroy patriotism
before that fatal day, were just as laughable
as their final predicament. This scene of the
Loyalist wits' venting their spleen upon the
unmoved structure of American liberty re-
minded him very much of a wasp endeavoring
to sting a church-steeple! Hear some lines
from his fable, *The Wasp:*

" Wrapt in Aurelian filth and slime,
    An infant wasp neglected lay;
Till having dosed the destined time,
    He woke and struggled into day.

. . . .

" ' In copious streams my spleen shall flow,
    And satire all her purses drain;
A critic born, the world shall know
    I carry not a sting in vain.'

" This said, from native cell of clay,
　　Elate he rose in airy flight;
Thence to the city changed his way,
　　And on a steeple chanced to light.

" ' Ye gods! ' he cried, ' what horrid pile
　　Presumes to rear his head so high?
This clumsy cornice—see how vile:
　　Can this delight a critic's eye? '

" With poisonous sting he strove to wound
　　The substance firm, but strove in vain;
Surprised he sees it stands its ground,
　　Nor starts through fear, nor writhes with pain.

" Away the enraged insect flew;
　　But soon with aggravated power,
Against the walls his body threw
　　And hoped to shake the lofty tower.

" Firm fixed it stands, as stand it must,
　　Nor heeds the wasp's unpitied fall:
The humbled critic rolls in dust,
　　So stunned, so bruised, he scarce can crawl."

Is it not clear how genuinely useful such a man was in those discouraging times? Many of the colonial leaders seemed instinctively to look to Francis Hopkinson whenever any faction or individual became too prominent in hostility, and Hopkinson seldom failed to squelch the troublesome party. How skilfully, for example, he checked that malicious enemy of independence, Provost Smith of the College of Philadelphia. The provost was writing in the *Pennsylvania Gazette* his dangerous *Letters of Cato to the People of Pennsylvania*. The people were more than interested—they were aroused; for the papers were strong in argument and forceful in style. An answer was needed and that right early. Hopkinson came to the rescue with *A Prophecy*. An ancient seer had a vision of what would occur, and did occur, in Philadelphia in 1776, and Hopkinson, it seems, interviewed the seer. It turned the laugh on the college president. After speaking of a tree sent over by the king of certain islands—a tree which proved exceedingly rotten at the core, the narration states that a proposal was made by a prophet (Dr. Franklin), to cut it down.

" And the people shall hearken to the voice of their prophet, for his sayings shall be good in their eyes. And they shall take up every man his spade and his axe, and shall prepare to dig up and cut away the shattered remains of the blasted and rotten tree, according to the words of their prophet.

" Then a certain wise man shall arise and shall call himself Cato; and he shall strive to persuade the people to put their trust in the rotten tree and not to dig it up or remove it from its place. And he shall harangue with great vehemence, and shall tell them that a rotten tree is better than a sound one; and that it is for the benefit of the people that the North wind should blow upon it, and that the branches thereof should be broken and fall upon and crush them.

" And he shall receive from the king of the islands fetters of gold and chains of silver; and he shall have hopes of great reward if he will fasten them on the necks of the people, and chain them to the trunk of the rotten tree. . . . And he shall tell the people that they are not fetters and chains, but shall be as bracelets of gold on their wrists, and rings of silver on their necks to ornament and decorate them and their children. And his words shall be sweet in the mouth, but very bitter in the belly.

.   .   .   .

" And it shall come to pass that certain other wise men shall also stand up and oppose themselves to Cato; and shall warn the people not to trust in the allurements of his voice, nor to be terrified with his threats, and to hearken to his puns no more. . . . And they shall earnestly exhort the people to despise

and reject the fetters of gold and the chains of silver
which the king of the islands would fasten upon them.

. . . .

"And in process of time the people shall root up
the rotten tree, and in its place they shall plant a
young and vigorous tree, and shall effectually defend
it from the winds of the North by an high wall. . . .
And the young tree shall grow and flourish and spread
its branches far abroad; and the people shall dwell
under the shadow of its branches, and shall become
an exceedingly great and powerful and happy nation. . . . "

Hopkinson's was a never ceasing pen for the
American cause. We have touched only here
and there in his works, and some of his best
efforts must be left unnoticed. It would be
pleasant to linger, for instance, over his *First
Book of the American Chronicle* or his odd
Specimens of a Modern Law Suit, wherein a
man is brought to trial for paring his nails on
Friday. It would be interesting, too, to look
over his mock advertisement of the Tory editor,
James Rivington, for whom circumstances had
"rendered it convenient . . . to remove to
Europe." Rivington had, for *immediate* sale,
various books, maps, and patent medicines,

some of which, according to Hopkinson, were as follows:

" The History of the American War; or the Glorious Exploits of the British Generals, Gage, Howe, Burgoyne, Cornwallis, and Clinton."

" The Right of Great Britain to the Dominion of the Sea—a Poetical Fiction."

" The State of Great Britain in October, 1760, and in October, 1781, compared and contrasted."

" Tears of Repentance: or the Present State of the Loyal Refugees in New York, and elsewhere."

" The Political Liar: a Weekly Paper, published by the Subscriber [Rivington], bound in Volumes."

" The Battle of Saratoga, and the Surrender at York: Two elegant Prints, cut in Copper, and dedicated to the King."

" Microscopes for magnifying small objects, furnished with a select set ready fitted for use. Amongst these are a variety of real and supposed successes of the British Generals in America."

" Pocket Glasses for Short-sighted Politicians."

" Vivifying Balsam: excellent for weak nerves, palpitation of the heart, over-bashfulness, and diffidence. In great demand for the officers of the army."

" Sp. Men. Or the genuine Spirit of Lying. Extracted by distillation from many hundreds of ' The Royal Gazette of New York.' "

" Anodyne Elixir, for quieting fears and apprehensions. Very necessary for Tories in all parts of America."

Few, indeed, were the men who served the American cause better than this "pretty, little, curious, ingenious gentleman," Francis Hopkinson. When he picked up his quill, well might the Tories lay in a supply of "Anodyne Elixir, for quieting fears and apprehensions." For to his task Hopkinson brought as keen an intellect, as great a degree of culture, and as forceful and witty a style as could be found in America, and his opponents often feared his good-humored ridicule far more than the violent and bitter expressions of some of his fellow patriots.

VIII

PHILIP FRENEAU

Some of the sweetest and most delicate verses in the earlier literature of America were written by a man whom the British and American Tories of colonial days considered nothing more nor less than a human wasp. The wasp was Philip Freneau (1752–1832). We of to-day know him mainly through three well-written bits of poetry, *Eutaw Springs*, *The Indian Burying-Ground*, and *The Wild Honey-Suckle*, and these three, it would seem, are not likely soon to be omitted from any thorough anthology of American poetry. Sir Walter Scott showed his admiration for *Eutaw Springs* when he used with but a slight change a line from it in the introduction to Canto III. of *Marmion:*

" And took the spear, but left the shield."

Campbell, in his *O'Connor's Child,* used, without any acknowledgments whatever, the beautiful idea embodied in the line from *The Indian Burying-Ground:*

> " The hunter still the deer pursues,
>   *The hunter and the deer—a shade.*"

Again, his *Death Song of a Cherokee Indian* was stolen almost bodily by an English woman, Mrs. Anna Hunter, and was praised by English critics as the best poem in a collection entitled *Specimens of British Poetesses.*

Freneau was a born poet and in a better day undoubtedly would have done lasting work. Like Pope, he " lisped in numbers, for the numbers came." At sixteen he wrote a long and ambitious poem, *The Prophet Jonah;* while at seventeen, he had the audacity to compose a dramatic piece in blank verse on so vast a subject as *The Pyramids of Egypt.* And portions of this juvenile work are indeed excellent. While a college boy of eighteen he wrote a poem called *The Power of Fancy;* and who would deny it an originality, a freshness of treatment rare indeed in that period of the eighteenth century?

171

" Lo! she walks upon the moon,
Listens to the chimy tune
Of the bright harmonious spheres,
And the song of angels hears;
Sees this earth a distant star,
Pendent, floating in the air;
Leads me to some lonely dome,
Where Religion loves to come,
Where the bride of Jesus dwells,
And the deep-toned organ swells
In notes with lofty anthems joined—
Notes that half distract the mind.

     .   .   .   .   .   .

" Fancy, thou the Muses' pride,
In thy painted realms reside
Endless images of things
Fluttering each on golden wings.

     .   .   .   .   .   .

Fancy, to thy power I owe
Half my happiness below;
By thee Elysian groves were made,
Thine were the notes that Orpheus played;
By thee was Pluto charmed so well
While rapture seized the sons of hell;
Come, O come, perceived by none,
You and I will walk alone."

And this came, remember, before Scott and
Wordsworth had revived the stiffened Muse of

the English people. With this freedom from conventionalities, there was in the man's make-up something of that daintiness which calls to mind the Cavalier singers of the seventeenth century. It may be seen—and, in addition, a genuine love of nature—in *The Wild Honey-Suckle:*

> " Fair flower, that dost so comely grow,
>   Hid in this silent, dull retreat,
> Untouched thy honeyed blossoms blow,
>   Unseen thy little branches greet;
> No roving foot shall find thee here,
> No busy hand provoke a tear.
>
> · · · · · · ·
>
> " From morning suns and evening dews
>   At first thy little being came;
> If nothing once, you nothing lose,
>   For when you die you are the same;
> The space between is but an hour,
> The frail duration of a flower."

The same daintiness, with not a few happy little conceits, may be seen in *The Parting Glass, A Lady's Singing Bird, On the Ruins of a Country Inn,* and *To a Honey Bee.* Some time, when you are in a sentimental mood, read these, and you will be surprised and delighted at their delicacy. As we see the bee light upon the tippler's glass of wine and drink, there comes with the half sad, half humorous sentiments of Freneau an echo of old Omar Khayyam sitting before the inn door of long ago.

> " Welcome!—I hail you to my glass;
> All welcome here you find;
> Here let the cloud of trouble pass,
> Here be all care resigned.
> This fluid never fails to please,
> And drown the grief of men or bees.''

And the bee having drowned himself:

> " Do as you please, your will is mine;
> Enjoy it without fear,
> And your grave will be this glass of wine,
> Your epitaph—a tear.
> Go, take your seat in Charon's boat;
> We'll tell the hive, you died afloat.''

But this is not the Freneau that we are to discuss. His was " an age employed in pointing steel,'' as he himself declared, and to pierce the enemy of his country with the pointed steel was the chief purpose of his life,—a purpose worth more in his estimation than all the fantastic and pretty creations of his poetic nature. Perhaps, if some brief account of his life be given, we can understand better the reasons for his choice, and why he was the poet of hatred rather than of love.

Freneau was born in New York in 1752. His ancestors were French Protestant refugees, and all his family had been cultivated, serious minded, and versatile people. His father, who was a wine merchant, was a man of considerable means, and he saw to it that the boy received a broad training. Young Freneau graduated at Princeton in 1771, and at that youthful age showed his fiery patriotism by reciting with another young fire-eater and humorist, Hugh Brackenridge, a dialogue entitled *The Rising Glory of America*.

And now began a most energetic career. Journalist, editor, trader, sea-captain, government official, farmer, poet, he lived the " strenuous life " with a zeal that would have satisfied even our greatest modern advocate of this form of existence. By 1775 he had gained notoriety by at least two compositions, *A Voyage to Boston* (1774) and *General Gage's Confession* (1775)—works which were soon to be followed by a consuming flood of vitriolic satires. In 1776 and 1780 he made voyages to the West Indies, with the result that, having been harassed on the first and captured on the second trip and thrust into a British prison-ship, he gained the good will of all American patriots by writing some of the most caustic sarcasm ever composed in any language. During the war many of his contributions appeared in the Philadelphia *Freeman's Journal;* in 1790 he was editor of the New York *Daily Advertiser;* and in 1791 he took charge of *The National Gazette* of Philadelphia. But he ever had a longing for the ocean—he shows it time after time in his poems—and between the years 1798 and 1812 he was back in the old sea-faring life. After 1812, he lived quietly at his home near Monmouth, New Jersey, and there it was that he lost his way one dark wintry night and was found dead in the snow.

The very fact that a man at the age of eighty-one would attempt to walk at a late hour of night through a wild, snow-covered waste, shows the energy, the self-reliance, the undauntedness of his nature. Tyler, in his *Literary History of the American Revolution,* gives a pen-picture of him at this age—a description well worth repeating: " He was still a fine specimen of active and manly old age; in person somewhat below the ordinary height, but muscular and compact; his face pensive in expression and with a care-worn look; his dark gray eyes sunken deep in their sockets, but sending out gleams and flashes of fire when aroused in talk; his hair once abundant and beautiful now thinned and bleached by time; stooping a little as he walked; to those who knew him, accustomed to give delight by a conversation abounding in anecdotes of the great age of the American Revolution."

This, then, was the most powerful of Revolutionary satirists, the most vehemently in earnest, the most unrelenting in his hatred. At times he could be playful; but it was the playfulness of a tiger. Beneath the softness were cruel claws and a merciless heart. Even in his mere playing they were not wholly concealed. Read his *Crispin O'Connor's Answer* and see why the Irishman came to America:

" In British land what snares are laid!—
There royal rights all right defeat:
They taxed my sun, they taxed my shade,
They taxed the wretched crumbs I eat;

" They taxed my hat, they taxed my shoes,
  Fresh taxes still on taxes grew;
  They would have taxed my very nose,
  Had I not fled, dear friends, to you! "

Even in those humorous verses not dealing
with Revolutionary themes, such as the *Song
of Thyrsis* in his *Female Frailty,* your sentiments and ideals are liable to get scratched.
Note how quickly the young widow recovers
from her bereavement, and begins, as Freneau
would doubtless have said in our own days, to
" sit up and take notice."

" The turtle on yon withered bough,
  That lately mourned her murdered mate,
  Has found another comrade now—
  Such changes all await!
  Again her drooping plume is drest,
  Again she's willing to be blest,
  And takes her lover to her nest.

" If nature has decreed it so
  With all above and all below,
  Let us, like them, forget our woe,
  And not be killed with sorrow.
  If I should quit your arms to-night
  And chance to die before 'twas light,
  I would advise you—and you might—
      Love again to-morrow."

Even in a playful poem on the wounding of his dog, Sancho, Freneau cannot resist the temptation to give a thrust. The poet's cabin had been attacked by robbers; the dog had rushed to its defence; and like that more famous dog, Bingo of the college song, he had soon been "cut up into sausage-meat."

" The world, my dear Sancho, is full of distress,
And you have your share, I allow and confess;
For twice with a musket, and now a cutteau—
You had nearly gone off to dog-heaven below.

. . . .

" Poor fellow, I pity your pitiful case!
In fact they have ruined the round of your face;
And die when you will, be it early or late,
You will go to your grave with a scar on your pate.

" If ever a dog be permitted to pass
Where folks I could mention have fixed on a place,
(*But which, I suspect, they will hardly attain
While rights of pre-emption in Satan remain.*)

" Good Sancho had merit to put in his plea,
And claim with the claimants a portion in fee,
On the ground that in life he was one of the few
Who, in watching and barking, were trusty and
      true."

We may say, however, that when Freneau
wrote such things he was not in normal condition. His temperature was entirely too low.
Between 1775 and 1780 he preferred fever-heat,
and he succeeded very easily in keeping himself
at that degree. Well might he exclaim:

" Rage gives me wings, and, fearless, prompts me on
To conquer brutes the world would blush to own;
No peace, no quarter, to such imps I lend—
Death and perdition on each line I send."

A man strong in his likes and dislikes and
always positive in his opinions, he generally
wrote what the spirit moved him to write, and
the spirit was never a hesitating one. In 1782,
after the Americans had shown King George
that they could not be conquered, Freneau wrote
his *Prophecy,* and there is no uncertainty in
the prophetic tones:

" When a certain great king, whose initial is G,
Shall force stamps upon paper, and folks to drink
tea;
When these folks burn his tea and stampt paper,
like stubble,
You may guess that this king is then coming to
trouble.

But when a petition he treads under his feet,
And sends over the ocean an army and fleet;
When that army, half-starved and frantic with rage,
Shall be cooped up with a leader whose name
  rhymes with cage;
When that leader goes home dejected and sad,
You may then be assured that the king's prospects
  are bad.
But when B and C with their armies are taken,
This king will do well if he saves his own bacon.
In the year seventeen hundred and eighty and two
A stroke he shall get that will make him look blue;
In the years eighty-three, eighty-four, eighty-five
You hardly shall know that the king is alive;
In the year eighty-six the affair will be over.
And he shall eat turnips that grow in Hanover.
The face of the Lion shall then become pale,
He shall yield fifteen teeth and be sheared of his
  tail.
O king, my dear king, you shall be very sore;
The Stars and the Lily shall run you on shore,
And your Lion shall growl—but never bite more!''

True, part of this prophecy was merely a
narrative of what had already happened; but
if Freneau had written it five years before there
would have been not a whit less positiveness.

It was in 1775 that we had from Freneau
the first ferocious outburst of patriotic ire.

181

Among the poems written that year by his rest-
less pen are such bitter satires as *On the Conquest of America Shut Up in Boston, General
Gage's Soliloquy, The Midnight Consultations,
Libera Nos, Domine,* and *Mac Swiggen*—
venomous things every one, especially poisonous to Tories. See what delight is his when
Gage is besieged in Boston by those American
" peasants " whom the general had denounced
and sworn to hang:

" ' Rebels you are '—the British champion cries—
Truth, stand you forth, and tell Tom Gage he lies!
' Rebels! '—and see, this mock imperial Lord
Already threats those ' rebels ' with the cord!

" The hour draws nigh, the glass is almost run,
When truth must shine and scoundrels be undone,
When this base miscreant shall forbear to sneer—
And curse his taunts and bitter insults here."

After reading his *Midnight Consultations,* we
may well imagine what a furore it made among
the Tories of New York, Philadelphia, and Boston. They were already sorely aggrieved at
the stubbornness of these plebeian colonists and
the lack of perseverance in the character of the
English regulars; and Freneau's satire was
acid poured upon their smarting wounds. The

poem tells of a meeting of British officers at
midnight after the Battle of Bunker Hill, at
which meeting confusion and anger reigned.
The officers were trying to devise a plan for
holding the slippery Americans:

" Twelve was the hour—congenial darkness reigned,
  And no bright star a mimic daylight feigned.
  First, Gage we saw—a crimson chair of state
  Received the honor of his Honor's weight.
  This man of straw the regal purple bound,
  But dullness, deepest dullness, hovered round.
  Next Graves, who wields the trident of the brine,
  The tall arch-captain of the embattled line,
  All gloomy sate—mumbling of flame and fire,
  Balls, cannons, ships, and all their damned attire;
  Well pleased to live in never-ending hum,
  But empty as the interior of his drum.
  Hard by, Burgoyne assumes an ample space,
  And seemed to meditate with studious face,

      .   .   .   .

  Is he to conquer—he subdue our land—
  This buckram hero, with his lady's hand?
  By Cæsars to be vanquished is a curse,
  But by a scribbling fop—by heaven, is worse!
  Lord Percy seemed to snore—but may the muse
  This ill-timed snoring to the peer excuse:
  Tired was the long boy of his toilsome day—
  Full fifteen miles he fled, a tedious way."

183

Gage's wrath was great. Thrice he swore, and cried:

        " ' 'Tis nonsense to be beat!
Thus to be drubbed! Pray, warriors, let me know
Which be in fault, myself, the fates, or you!
Hencefore let Britain deem her men mere toys!
Gods! to be frighted thus by country boys.
Why, if our army had a mind to sup,
They might have eat that schoolboy army up!

    .   .   .   .

You have the knack, Lord Percy, to retreat;
The death you 'scaped my warmest blood congeals,
Heaven grant me, too, so swift a pair of heels! ' "

And there too was that meagre—tearfully meagre—fare! How could it longer be borne by a high-born British officer? " Three weeks," cried Gage,

" ' Three weeks—ye gods! nay, three long years it
    seems,
Since roast beef I have touched, except in dreams.
In sleep choice dishes to my view repair,—
Waking I gaze and champ the empty air.
Say, is it just that I, who rule these bands,
Should live on husks, like rakes in foreign lands?—
Come, let us plan some project ere we sleep,
And drink destruction to the rebel sheep.

On neighboring isles uncounted cattle stray,
Fat beeves and swine—an ill defended prey;
These are fit victims for my noonday dish,
These, if my soldiers act as I would wish,
In one short week would glad your maws and mine—
On mutton we will sup, on roast beef dine! '
Shouts of applause re-echoed through the hall,
And what pleased one as surely pleased them all;
Wallace was named to execute the plan,
And thus sheep-stealing pleased them to a man."

Mention has been made of another sarcastic poem of Freneau's written in 1775—his *Libera Nos, Domine*. In but one other piece, *The Prison Ship*, of which we shall hear later, is his denunciation more biting, his nauseating disgust more apparent. How vividly and how vehemently he sums up in this mock litany the woes of his country and the tyranny of Britain. Lord, deliver us, he cries,

" From the group at St. James's that slight our petitions,
  And fools that are waiting for further submissions;
  From a nation whose manners are rough and abrupt,
  From scoundrels and rascals whom gold can corrupt;

. . . .

" From the valiant Dunmore, with his crew of ban-
      ditti,
  Who plunder Virginians at Williamsburgh city;
  From hot-headed Montague, mighty to swear,
  The little fat man with his pretty white hair.

                . . . .

" From Tyron the mighty, who flies from our city,
  And swelled with importance, disdains the com-
      mittee,—
  (But since he is pleased to proclaim us his foes,
  What the devil care we where the devil he goes) ;

" From the scoundrel, Lord North, who would bind us
      in chains,
  From a dunce of a king who was born without
      brains,
  The utmost extent of whose sense is to see
  That reigning and making of buttons agree;

" From an island that bullies and hectors and swears,
  I send up to heaven my wishes and prayers
  That we, disunited, may freemen be still,
  And Britain go on—to be damned, if she will! "

It is rather surprising to find that this hydro-
phobic fire-eater joined no regiment, commanded no war-vessel, engaged in no physical
strife whatever with the British foe. His writings clearly show that he could not have be-
longed to the class stigmatized by Tom Paine

as " the summer soldier and the sunshine patriot; " but why did he not enter into actual
warfare? Doubtless we shall never know.
The Americans may have considered him more
valuable to the cause while he was at his desk
than in the field. There are some unaccount-
able lapses even in his satirical warfare—
periods when he wrote almost nothing for the
amusement of the " home folks " and the instruction of the foreigners. We have noted
that in 1776 he sailed for the West Indies, where
he remained until the middle of 1778, and on
those islands he composed some of his longest,
most imaginative, and most nearly perfect
works. But they do not, however, deal with
rebellious colonists. By 1778 he was back in
the colonies and at his old work of sending
forth scornful invectives against the red-coats.
Exulting that America had declared her independence, he wrote his *America Independent
and Her Everlasting Deliverance from British
Tyranny and Oppression.* How many a compliment of vinegar flavor King George and his
Tory advisers received in this energetic
tirade! Looking upon the Royalists, Freneau
thus expressed himself:

" So vile a crew the world ne'er saw before,
And grant, ye pitying heavens, it may no more!
If ghosts from hell infest our poisoned air,
Those ghosts have entered these base bodies here.

. . . .

Whene'er they wed, may demons and despair
And grief and woe and blackest night be there;
Fiends leagued from hell the nuptial lamp display,
Swift to perdition light them on their way,
Round the wide world their devilish squadrons
        chase—
To find no realm that grants one resting place."

Then, where. and when shall Tories find their
resting place? Freneau finds but one suitable
spot:

" Far to the North, on Scotland's utmost end,
An isle there lies, the haunt of every fiend;
There screeching owls and screaming vultures rest,
And not a tree adorns its barren breast.

. . . .

Shrouded in ice, the blasted mountains show
Their cloven heads, to fright the seas below:

. . . .

The blackening wind, incessant storms prolong,
Dull as their night, and dreary as my song.
When stormy winds with rain refuse to blow,
Then from the dark sky drives the unpitying snow;

. . . .

188

No peace, no rest, the elements bestow,
But seas forever rage, and storms forever blow.

" Here, miscreants, here with Loyal hearts retire,
Here pitch your tents, and kindle here your fire;
Here desert nature will her stings display,
And fiercest hunger on your vitals prey."

Another lapse now occurred in Freneau's literary productiveness; but it was only a lull before the hurricane. In 1780, evidently weary of war and its demands, he again shipped for the West Indies; but he had scarcely gotten out to sea when a British ship bore down upon his vessel, captured all, and carried him a prisoner to New York. Imprisoned in a " rotten hulk," *The Scorpion,* he literally suffered the torments of hell, gained relief in the unconsciousness of a raging fever, and awoke to find himself in a hospital ship, *The Hunter.* If his bemuddled brain had conceived the idea that a hospital ship would present any fewer horrors than *The Scorpion,* he was very soon and very rudely undeceived. Never did he forget those days of suffering. In his poem dealing with the experience, *The British Prison Ship* (1780), he cried to the American sailors:

" Strike not your standards to this miscreant foe.
  Better the greedy wave should swallow all,
  Better to meet the death-conducted ball,
  Better to sleep on ocean's deepest bed,
  At once destroyed and numbered with the dead,
  Than thus to perish in the face of day—
  Where twice ten-thousand deaths one death repay.''

Remembrance followed him everywhere; he
was literally full of the " Scorpion " poison.
He saw in his dreams the beasts in human form
that walked the deck of the cursed vessel:

" Still in my view some English brute appears—
  Some base-born Hessian slave walks threat'ning
    by—
  Some servile Scot, with murder in his eye,
  Still haunts my sight, as vainly they bemoan
  Rebellions managed so unlike their own!

" Oh may I never feel the poignant pain,
  To live subjected to such fiends again,—
  Stewards and mates that hostile Britain bore,
  Cut from the gallows on their native shore,—
  Their ghastly looks and vengeance—beaming eyes
  Still to my view in dismal colors rise.

    ·   ·   ·   ·   ·   ·   ·   ·   ·

  Hunger and thirst to work our woe combine,
  And mouldy bread, and flesh of rotten swine,
  The mangled carcase, and the battered brain,

The doctor's poison, and the captain's cane,
The soldier's musket, and the steward's debt,
The evening shackle, and the noon-day threat!

. . . .

Shut from the blessings of the evening air,
Pensive we lay with mangled corpses there;
Meagre and wan and scorched with heat, below,
We loomed like ghosts, ere death had made us so! "

One figure stands out before most of the others in cruelty and savagery—the Hessian doctor. " Fair Science never called the wretch her son." Many an American soldier in wars much more modern than the Revolution can appreciate the truth if not the humor of this description of the blundering quack:

" He on his charge the healing work begun
With antimonial mixtures—by the tun;

. . . .

He drenched us well with bitter draughts, 'tis true,
Nostrums from Hell, and cortex from Peru;
Some with his pills he sent to Pluto's reign,
And some he blistered with his flies of Spain;
His Cream of Tartar walked its deadly round,
Till the lean patient at the potion frowned,
And swore that hemlock, death, or what you will,
Were nonsense to the drugs that stuffed his bill.

191

On those refusing, he bestowed a kick,
Or menaced vengeance with his walking-stick;
Here, uncontrolled, he exercised his trade,
And grew experienced by the deaths he made;
By frequent blows we from his cane endured,
He killed at least as many as he cured,
On our lost comrades built his future fame,
And scattered fate where'er his footsteps came.
Some did not seem obedient to his will,
And swore he mingled poison with his pill;
But I acquit him by a fair confession—
He was no Englishman—he was a Hessian!
Although a dunce, he had some sense of sin,
Or else—the Lord knows where we now had been,—
Perhaps in that far country sent to range
Where never prisoner meets with an exchange!"

After this experience in the prison-ship there was nevermore a sentiment of peace in Freneau's breast. He wrote like a frenzied man; his whole life seemed henceforth to be bent toward one purpose:—to show the British and the Tories their utter fitness for the land of brimstone and eternal damnation. Look, for a moment, at his *Political Balance, or the Fates of Britain and America Compared.* Jove, the king of all Creation, "happened to light on the records of Fate."

" In alphabet order this volume was written,
   So he opened at B., for the article ' Britain.'
   ' She struggles so well,' said the god, ' I will see
What the sisters in Pluto's dominions decree! '

" And first on the top of a column he read—
   ' Of a king with a mighty soft place in his head,
Who should join in his temper the ass and the mule,
The Third of his name, and by far the worst fool.

" ' His reign shall be famous for multiplication,
   The sire and the king of a whelp generation;
But such is the will and the purpose of Fate,
For each child he begets he shall forfeit a state.' "

This did not give Jove all the information desirable, and, in order that he might discover for himself the ultimate end of Great Britain, he ordered Vulcan to make him a globe representing the earth, so constructed that it might be taken apart and weighed in sections. Vulcan turned out a fine piece of work, and placed in it all the known geographical divisions.

" Adjacent to Europe he struck up an island,
   One part of it low, but the other was high land,
With many a comical creature upon it,
And one wore a hat, and another a bonnet.

   .   .   .   .

" These poor little creatures were all in a flame,
To the lands of America urging their claim,
Still biting or stinging or spreading their sails,—
For Vulcan had formed them with stings in their
    tails.
" So poor and so lean, you might count all their ribs,
Yet were so enraptured with crackers and squibs,
That Vulcan with laughter almost split asunder—
' Because they imagined their crackers were thun-
    der.' "

All being finished, Jove, with the aid of all
the gods, succeeded in lifting huge Columbia—
" one eighth of the globe "—into the scale; but
the effort cost the gods many a grunt. Then
Jove began to search for Great Britain.

" Then searching about with his fingers for Britain,
Thought he, ' This same island I cannot well hit on;
The devil take him who first called her the Great!
If she was—she is vastly diminished of late.'

" Like a man that is searching his thigh for a flea,
He peeped and he fumbled, but nothing could see;
At last he exclaimed—' I'm surely upon it—
I think I have hold of a highlander's bonnet.' "

By the aid, however, of two moons used as
glasses, he at length gains a clear view of the
islands:

" ' But, faith, she's so small I must mind how I shake
    her—
  In a box I'll enclose her, for fear I should break
    her:
  Though a god, I might suffer for being aggressor,
  Since scorpions and vipers and hornets possess her,

  .   .   .   .

" ' But, Vulcan, inform me what creatures are these
  That smell so of onions and garlic and cheese? '
  Old Vulcan replied—' Odds splutter a nails!
  Why these are the Welsh, and the country is Wales!
  When Taffy is vexed, no devil is ruder—
  Take care how you handle the offspring of Tudor! '

  .   .   .   .

" Jove peeped through his moons and examined their
    features,
  And said, ' By my troth, they are wonderful creat-
    ures!—
  The beards are so long they encircle their throats,
  That—unless they are Welshmen—I swear they are
    goats.

" ' But now, my dear Juno, pray give me my mit-
    tens—
  The insects I am going to handle are Britons—
  I'll draw up their isle with a finger and thumb,
  As the doctor extracts an old tooth from your gum.'

195

" Then he raised her aloft—but to shorten our tale—
She looked like a clod in the opposite scale,
Britannia so small, and Columbia so large—
A ship of first rate, and a ferryman's barge! "

Jove was disgusted.

" ' Then cease your endeavors, ye vermin of
        Britain '—
And here in derision their island he spit on—
' 'Tis madness to seek what you never can find,
Or think of uniting what nature disjoined;

" ' But still you may flutter awhile with your wings,
And spit out your venom, and brandish your stings;
Your hearts are as black and as bitter as gall—
A curse to yourselves, and a blot on the Ball! ' "

Here is a positive genius for rubbing the fur
the wrong way. Doubtless old King George,
if he ever read any of these tirades of Freneau,
must have felt like exclaiming, with another
foolish king, " How sharper than a serpent's
tooth is an unthankful child! " From such a
hater could we ever expect true reconciliation?
Even after George III had made his speech
recommending peace, Freneau arose in his
wrath and shouted:

196

" Monster!—no peace shall greet thy breast:
Our murdered friends shall never cease
To hover round and break thy rest!
The Furies shall thy bosom tear,
Remorse, Distraction, and Despair,
And Hell with all its fiends, be there!

" Cursed be the ship that e'er set sail
    Hence, freighted for thy odious shore;
May tempests o'er her strength prevail,
    Destruction round her roar!
May Nature all her aids deny,
    The sun refuse his light,
The needle from its object fly,
    No star appear by night,
        Till the base pilot, conscious of his crime,
        Directs the prow to some more grateful clime."

Freneau's was no hackneyed pen. He wrote
with his whole heart, and his heart was one
large mass of concentrated ire. With an
originality not equalled perhaps by any other
eighteenth century American writer, and with
a vigor worthy of his riotous times, he served
the colonial cause in a way no other man of
the age could have served it. A genuine lover
of the rights of man was this Philip Freneau;
not so rhetorical as Tom Paine, but undoubt-

197

edly more sincere, more savagely in earnest in his efforts to crush the enemies of liberty. He saw the possibilities of the nation, and believed, as he wrote, that

" The time shall come when strangers rule no more,
  Nor cruel mandates vex from Britain's shore;
  When commerce shall extend her shortened wing,
  And her rich freights from every climate bring;
  When mighty towns shall flourish free and great,—
  Vast their dominion, opulent their state;
  When one vast cultivated region teems
  From ocean's side to Mississippi's streams,
  While each enjoys his vine tree's peaceful shade
  And even the meanest has no foe to dread."

IX

JOHN TRUMBULL

We come now to the last of the more prominent wits of this battle of words,—John Trumbull (1750-1831). Tradition tells a pretty little story about that name. One of the kings
of England—the tradition is pleasantly in-
definite—while walking through a field, at-
tracted the attention of a bull who, it seems,
was not especially fond of kings. The vicious
creature rushed bellowing toward the ruler and
undoubtedly would soon have gored the royal
sprinter to death had not a peasant bravely
hastened to the rescue and battled for his High-
ness' life. The grateful king at once declared that henceforth the laborer's name
should be Turnbull, and, what was of more importance to the rustic, gave him a pension of
one hundred marks and a coat of arms co-
piously decorated with bulls' heads. Thus,
for a long time the name was Turnbull; but

some centuries after the incident a certain proud member of the family, fearing that his ancestry might be connected by the scornful with a butcher-shop, had the name changed to Trumbull, and so it has remained until this day.

Tales still more curious are told about the particular Trumbull now under our observation. It is declared, in his private papers, that before he was two he had memorized all the verses in the *Primer* and in Watts' *Divine Songs for Children;* at two and a half he could read readily; at five he had completed a reading of the Bible, and was composing verses of his own. Before he was six he had learned Latin and Greek by listening to his father's pupils, and at seven he passed the entrance examination for Yale! That this last mentioned point is a fact may be ascertained from the accounts given of it in the old files of various New England newspapers, notably *The Connecticut Gazette* of September, 1757. His father had the good sense, however, not to allow him to enter the college until he was thirteen.

What might we not expect from such a youth? That he would become either an idiot or a Macaulay. He became neither. So much for the caprices of nature. But he did develop into one of the most learned men of colonial America, certainly one of the keenest wits of his day, and the author of the only American mock-heroic poem that approaches the rank of *Mac Flecknoe* and *The Dunciad*. Before we progress further, however, perhaps we should note something of his life. It is but human nature to desire to know where a man was born, why he was born, and when he died.

John Trumbull came of what Emerson and Holmes called the Brahmin stock of New England. Born at Waterbury, Connecticut, in 1750, he was thoroughly, one might almost say, *violently,* educated by his father, and received the bachelor's degree from Yale in 1767 and the master's in 1770. If any reader has the idea that Yale was in this day a dull and gloomy cavern of asceticism and pessimistic theology, he is much mistaken. A gay and brilliant company of young men were within its walls, and there was a genuine love and interest for the purer forms of literature and the fine arts perhaps not equalled in that famous institution at this very moment. Here, it seems, Trumbull did his first published literary work. In

September, 1769, he began in the *Boston Chronicle* a series of essays named *The Meddler,—* and the name was indeed fitting. They meddled with everything that might interest a mortal being. Here indeed was pure love of writing. In spite of the fact that Trumbull declared his purpose to be " instructing the ignorant, diverting and improving the learned, rectifying the tastes and manners of the time, and cultivating the fine arts," we are tempted to believe that he wrote, just as many a writer has before and since, simply for the fun of writing. And the pleasure was not all his; those articles have an entertaining quality that survives to this day. Although too evidently modelled after the *Spectator,* they dispense very pleasantly with much of the circumlocution and primness of the classic English papers, and speak with a raciness and a vivacity that perhaps mark them as the lineal ancestor of the *Autocrat* series.

We may not here go into a detailed examination; for there are more important productions to be discussed; perhaps, however, this little advertisement from one of the " discourses " may give some idea of their piquant yet genial flavor:

THE HUMOR OF THE REVOLUTION

* " To Be Sold At Public Vendue,
   The Whole Estate of
Isabella Sprightly, Toast and Coquette,
   (*Now retiring from Business*).

" Imprimis, all the Tools and Utensils necessary for carrying on the Trade, viz: Several bundles of Darts and Arrows, well-pointed, and capable of doing great execution. A considerable quantity of Patches, Paint, Brushes, and Cosmetics, for plastering, painting, and whitewashing the face; a complete set of caps, ' a la mode a Paris,' of all sizes from five to fifteen inches in height; With several dozens of Cupids, very proper to be stationed on a ruby lip, a diamond eye, or a roseate cheek.

" Item, as she proposes by certain ceremonies to transform one of her humble servants into a husband, and keep him for her own use, she offers for sale, Florio, Daphnis, Cynthio, and Cleanthes, with several others, whom she won by a constant attendance on business during the space of four years. She can prove her indisputable right thus to dispose of them, by certain deeds of gifts, bills of sale, and attestation, vulgarly called love-letters, under their own hands and seals. They will be offered very cheap, for they are all of them broken-hearted, consumptive, or in a dying condition. Nay, some of them have been dead this half year, as they declare and testify in the above-mentioned writing.

---

* Copied from the Trumbull MSS. as given in Tyler's *Literary History of the American Revolution.*

" N.B. Their hearts will be sold separately."

Again, speaking of that bad habit of society folk, of being out late and arising long after the cock has crowed the healthful hour, he says:

" The Afternoon hath of late made great encroachments upon its neighbors, and strangely jostled and discomposed the other parts of the day. It hath driven forward the Morning from its proper station, and forced it to take refuge in the habitation of Noon; it hath made Breakfast and Dinner shake hands, and been the total destruction of Supper; it hath devoured a large portion of Night, and unless a speedy stop be put to its motion, may probably swallow up the whole four and twenty Hours."

It is evident that this college-student had the talent to become in time a writer of ability, and the fact was just as clear to the young man himself as to anybody else. The year he received his master's degree (1770) he began another series, *The Correspondent*, in the *Connecticut Journal and New Haven Post Boy*. We do not know why the editor did not amputate some portion of his paper's name; but we can readily see why he allowed Trumbull to contribute to his columns. This second series is a trifle more sarcastic than the first, and is written with a mock dignity and supercilious loftiness that make a sympathetic reader unconsciously raise his eyebrows, wag his head in gay unconcern, and try to act just as superciliously. The writer himself, however, was really—and perhaps unknown to himself—growing more earnest. He attacked various would-be philosophers, dogmatic divines of the day, and sundry ridiculous vagaries then becoming dangerously popular; and now and then he hit hard. Clearly this industrious college fellow was getting ready for the main work of his life.

After receiving his master's degree, Trumbull studied law a year; but in the fall of 1771 he was back at Yale as a tutor, and here we find him for the next two years. Evidently he was giving considerable time to a serious study of philosophy; for several of his published papers of this period deal with abstruse questions, and consequently are just about as interesting to the general reader as their subjects are. But the spirit of playfulness in the man would not down, in spite of the dignity expected of a Yale tutor, and in the second year of his work there we see him once more enjoying life in the preparation of a second series of

The Correspondent. At this time, too, appeared his first long satirical poem. *The Progress of Dulness,* published in 1772, was something of a revelation to American readers. Here was a man who could write lines not unworthy, at times, of Dryden and Pope. And how bitterly true this *Progress* was! Such a volume of protests as arose immediately after its publication had never before greeted an American poem. Surely the shoe must have more than fit; it must have pinched the tender New England foot. As to that, however, we each may judge for ourselves a little later in this discussion.

It now seemed to occur to Trumbull, as to many another college professor since, that if he intended ever to possess any of this world's goods he had better turn his wits to some other profession. In November, 1773, he was admitted to the bar of Connecticut, and from this time forth he looked to the law for his daily bread. Before, however, he began the actual practice of it, he went to Boston, where he studied with John Adams and lived in the home of another prominent man, Thomas Cushing. Doubtless this had much to do with arousing

that patriotic ire for which he afterwards became so noted, and also in shaping his future
career as a satirical opponent of Toryism and
all that savored of royal prerogative. Then,
too, he was in Boston when the strife first began
to assume astonishing proportions, when the
hastily arranged but highly successful Tea
Party was given, and when King George tried
so vainly to " bottle up " Boston and seal the
cork besides. (Critics will kindly excuse this
twentieth century expression; we must use a
few terms later than Johnson's day, else the
language will become petrified.) We must not
think, however, that Trumbull's interest in the
law made him forget his poetic talent. During
that year at Boston he composed three dignified,
even stern poems, *The Prophecy of Balaam*,
The Destruction of Babylon, and *An Elegy on
the Times, Composed at Boston during the
Operation of the Port Bill.* Needless to say,
among such environments his poems breathed
forth prophecies of dire disaster to England
and all her friends.

During the next year Trumbull settled down
to the serious practice of law. And in spite of
his frail health and the fact that he was known

as a humorist and not an especially dignified barrister, he was exceedingly successful, became State Attorney for Hartford County, a member of the legislature, a Judge of the Superior Court, and finally a Judge of the Supreme Court of Errors. But fickle is fame. Doubtless the folk of the times thought this man would long be remembered as a mighty judge in the land and that his scribblings of the Revolutionary days would soon pass into oblivion; and lo! not one person in ten thousand knows that he ever sat on the bench, while any high-school boy can tell you that he wrote *McFingal*.

But to return to that year at Boston. Just here is the turning point in Trumbull's career. He is now to sacrifice his ambition for a life devoted to pure literature. He is to offer his education, his culture, his genius, on the altar of his harassed country. Henceforth he is to be a satirist, a scoffing, ridiculing, boisterous maker of popular verse, instead of a creator of the noble poetry which he hoped and had the talent to write. That he did this, not through an itching for fame, but through genuine love of country, is evidenced in the fact that much of his work at this period was anonymous and none of it remunerative.

In August, 1775, he wrote for the *Connecticut Courant,* a burlesque on Gage's proclamation to the " rebels," and doubtless the applause which this effort received encouraged him to hasten his work on his masterpiece, *McFingal,* then under preparation. The first canto of this mock epic appeared in Philadelphia on almost the same day in January, 1776, as Tom Paine's vigorous treatise, *Commonsense.* Of course, John Trumbull wrote much after this date but the main literary work of his life was now done. In 1781, when the strain of war was practically over, he divided this first canto of *McFingal* into two, added two more, and in 1782 issued the poem in its present form. Henceforth busy with his duties as a lawyer and judge, he passed his life in industry and with undoubted usefulness to his countrymen. But the spark that might have become a flame of genius had perished, it seems, in the day of strife, and the poet that might have been remained merely the poet—that *might* have been. In 1825 the old man, a distinguished jurist by this time, decided to remove to Detroit to spend his last days with his daughter in that wilderness village. He tarried for a few days in New York City, where a great banquet was given him, and all the famous men of the day, it seems, gathered to bid him God-speed. At Detroit he lived the quiet, studious life of which he was always fond, and there in 1831 he died. A striking monument stands over his grave in Elmwood cemetery in that city.

Here was a man who, in a work which he declared uncongenial, surpassed any other American who has ever attempted the type of verse that made the fame of Dryden, Pope, Churchill, and a score of other poetic wits of Great Britain. In what traits does he surpass? It is necessary for our purpose here to examine but two of his works,—his masterpieces, *The Progress of Dulness* and *McFingal*.

As we have intimated, Trumbull did not believe himself a natural satirist. Commenting upon the question, he once wrote: " I was born the dupe of imagination. My satirical turn was not native. It was produced by the keen spirit of critical observation operating on disappointed expectation, and avenging itself on real or fancied wrongs." One cannot read *The*

Progress of Dulness without seriously doubting the statement. Even if not to the manner born, however, he would in all probability have been forced into satirical conflicts by the very spirit of the times. It was the fashion of the day to be a witty scribbler. That cross-grained genius, Pope, had cast his flippant slurs at all forms of humanity; Charles Churchill was stinging the reading world with a sharp and venomous pen; while a host of Grub Street slashers were exercising their ill-natured spleen. It paid to be satirists; men feared and endeavored to conciliate them.

Whatever the reason, it was not the Revolution that made Trumbull a merciless wit. *The Progress of Dulness,* written before the war, has a keenness, a precision in its thrusts, an accuracy of observation that show an unusual genius for saying sharp things in a sharp way. The poem deals with three phases of intellectual poverty—a poverty just as prevalent to-day as in the eighteenth century. First come the adventures of Tom Brainless, wherein the forms of education offered by American colleges of Trumbull's day are arraigned and proved to be as useless as some phases of the modern system. Tom, the farmer's son, must go to college. He has shown no particular aptitude for study,—in fact, he is something of a blockhead; but his parents have made the decree, and to college Tom must go. In the institution he is soon overcome by that most prevalent college disease—laziness.

" Greek spoils his eyes, the print's so fine,
  Grown dim with study, or with wine;
  Of Tully's Latin much afraid,
  Each page he calls the doctor's aid;
  While geometry with lines so crooked,
  Sprains all his wits to overlook it.
  His sickness puts on every name,
  Its cause and uses still the same,—
  'Tis tooth-ache, colic, gout, or stone,
  With phases various as the moon;
  But though through all the body spread,
  Still makes its cap'tal seat, the head.
  In all diseases, 'tis expected,
  The weakest parts be most infected.
  Kind Head-Ache, hail! thou blest disease,
  The friend of idleness and ease;
  Who, mid the still and dreary bound
  Where college walls her sons surround,
  In spite of fears, in justice 'spite,
  Assum'st o'er laws dispensing right,
  Set'st from his task the blunderer free,
  Excused by dullness and by thee."

Other students work hard.

> " And plodding on in one dull tone,
> Gain ancient tongues and lose their own."

Tom, however, is in no such danger.

At length the young dunce comes forth with his diploma; how he obtained it is one of those mysteries known only to weary faculties and college presidents. See the fledgling Solomon, as he disdainfully mingles with the stupid populace.

> " Our hero's wit and learning now may
> Be proud by token of diploma,
> Of that diploma which with speed
> He learns to construe and to read;
> And stalks abroad with conscious stride,
> In all the airs of pedant pride,
> With passport sign'd for wit and knowledge
> And current under seal of college."

But, alas,

> " Few months now past, he sees with pain,
> His purse as empty as his brain."

His father advises him " to teach a school at first and then to preach," and Tom promptly decides to become a teacher. This is, of course, the most natural thing in the world, as school-boards are frequently seeking cheap blockheads, and such fellows seldom fail to secure the position if they sell their ignorance lower than other blockheads.

Tom is a great success; he can wield the rod's "electric end" with wonderful agility. But the real ambition of his life is to become a preacher. He studies theology and

> " Learns with nice art to make with ease
> The Scriptures speak whate'er he please;
> With judgment, unperceived, to quote
> What Poole explained, or Henry wrote;
> To give the gospel new editions,
> Split doctrines into propositions,
> Draw motives, uses, inferences,
> And torture words in thousand senses;
> Learn the grave style and goodly phrase,
> Safe handed down from Cromwell's days,
> And shun, with anxious Care the while,
> The infection of a modern style! "

Thus equipped, he goes forth to find a flock, discovers it in a withered, or more accurately speaking, a petrified country-town, sinks into a living oblivion,

" And starves on sixty pounds a year;
And culls his texts, and tills his farm,
Does little good and little harm;
On Sunday, in his best array,
Deals forth the dullness of the day;
And while above he spends his breath,
The yawning audience nod beneath.''

Behold what wonders education hath wrought!
Thus endeth the story of Tom Brainless.

The second part of *The Progress of Dulness*
tells of one, Dick Hairbrain, and is a really
strong piece of writing dealing with a subject
which is still paramount in college circles—the
evil life of the money-cursed, pampered, and
sensual college boy. The third part of the
poem is even more modern. In fact, we have
not even yet reached the high plane of some of
the views expressed in this treatise in verse.
Miss Harriet Simper shows us, by her
ignorance, silliness, and empty life, the folly of
giving women no deeper and higher insight
into knowledge, of excluding her from the
realm of higher thought, and of condemning
her to a shallow, narrow round of existence.
What a fate is Harriet's, and yet how common
a one!

" Poor Harriet now hath had her day;
No more the beaux confess her sway;
New beauties push her from the stage;
She trembles at th' approach of age,
And starts to view the alter'd face
That wrinkles at her in her glass.
So Satan, in the monk's tradition,
Feared when he met his apparition.
At length her name each coxcomb cancels
From standing lists of toasts and angels;
And slighted where she shone before,
A grace and goddess now no more.
Despised by all, and doomed to meet
Her lovers at her rival's feet,
She flies assemblies, shuns the ball,
And cries out, vanity, on all;
Affects to scorn the tinsel-shows
Of glittering belles and gaudy beaux

   .   .   .   .   .

Now careless grown of airs polite,
Her noonday nightcap meets the sight;
Her hair uncomb'd collects together
With ornaments of many a feather

   .   .   .   .   .

A careless figure half undress'd
(The reader's wits may guess the rest);

   .   .   .   .   .

She spends her breath, as years prevail,
At this sad, wicked world to rail,
To slander all her sex impromptu,
And wonder what the times will come to. ''

This, be it remembered, is not a crude production of an uncultured provincial. There is an admirable finish in much of it, and, with this polish, an artistic unity, a keen observation, a power of sustaining, and an ability to produce epigram not unworthy, at times, of Pope himself.

Well conceived and well written as this is, *McFingal* is a much more masterly production. In this we approach, perhaps at times even equal, the excellence of the *Dunciad, Mac Flecknoe,* and portions of the *Rape of the Lock.* Griswold once said that it was the best imitation of Butler's *Hudibras* that had been written; but if this really is an imitation of the famous English satire, here is an instance where the imitation excels at many points the original. It can make no claim to be noble or beautiful poetry; but it has that saving grace which every successful satire must possess,— energy, and withal a kind of verse which, while not accurate in its metre and rhyme, compels a smile through its agility.

For those who have not read the poem there awaits what the modern editor calls " a rattling good story." Squire McFingal, a Scotch-American living in a provincial town, believed heartily in absolute submission to Parliament. The Squire was a most windy orator, ready to speak on any subject or occasion; but his chief power lay in telling in thunderous tones just what would happen if Americans did not behave better. He

> " Brought armies o'er by sudden pressings
> Of Hanoverians, Swiss, and Hessians;
> Feasted with blood his Scottish clan,
> And hang'd all rebels, to a man;
> Divided their estates and pelf,
> And took a goodly share himself."

Now, Squire McFingal's chief rival in the town was a certain patriot named Honorius. In the course of colonial events a town-meeting was held in which Honorius made a fiery harangue to the citizens. In the midst of the speech the Squire came in frowning severely, and took a seat near the orator; but Honorius, not a whit abashed, continued his loud-voiced discourse. " Britain," shouted he,

> " . . . midst her airs so flighty,
> Now took a whim to be almighty;
> Urged on to desperate heights of **frenzy**,
> Affirmed her own omnipotency;
> Would rather ruin all her race
> Than 'bate supremacy an ace."

When Americans protested, he declared, England

> " Then signed her warrants of ejection,
> And gallows raised to stretch our necks on;
> And on these errands sent in rage,
> Her bailiff and her hangman, Gage;
> And at his heels, like dogs to bait us,
> Despatched her ' posse comitatus.' "

And who is this mighty Gage? What powers are his? What strength of intellect, culture, followers, resources?

> " And as old heroes gained by shifts,
> From gods, as poets tell, their gifts,
> Our general, as his actions show,
> Gained like assistance from below,—
> By Satan graced with full supplies
> From all his magazine of lies."

Then the wrathful Honorius turned upon the Squire himself and called that stern-faced Tory the leader of a party composed of

> " Priests who, if Satan should sit down
> To make a Bible of his own,
> Would gladly, for the sake of mitres,
> Turn his inspired and sacred writers;
> Lawyers who, should he wish to prove
> His title t' his old seat above,

219

Would, if his cause he'd give 'em fees in
Bring writs of ' Entry sur disseisin,'
Plead for him boldly at the session,
And hope to put him in possession;
Merchants who, for his kindly aid,
Would make him partners in their trade;
And judges who would list his pages
For proper liveries and wages."

McFingal could stand no more. Arising in
his wrath, he made a few preliminary remarks
and then entered, as usual, into a hair-raising
prophecy. " Behold! " he cried,

" Behold the world will stare at new sets
Of home-made Earls in Massachusetts;
Admire, arrayed in ducal tassels,
Your Ol'vers, Hutchinsons, and Vassals;

  . . . . . .

In wide-sleeved pomp of goodly guise,
What solemn rows of bishops rise!
Aloft a Card'nal's hat is spread
O'er punster Cooper's rev'rend head!

  . . . . . .

Knights, viscounts, barons shall ye meet
As thick as pavements in the street!
Even I, perhaps—Heaven speed my claim—
Shall fix a Sir before my name."

But these new-fangled notions cannot be victorious. The so-called patriots will soon be hewers of wood and drawers of water.

> " The vulgar knaves
> Will do more good preserved as slaves."

Affairs now became decidedly exciting. Honorius replied to the Squire's speech, but was interrupted by some Tory rowdies, and the meeting bid fair to terminate in a free-for-all fight. Luckily, however, a loud disturbance outside suddenly drew the people's attention, and the meeting adjourned *sine die*.

Here the original McFingal story closed. But, as we have seen, Trumbull in 1782 published the poem enlarged into four cantos, and in this version we find, to our great satisfaction, that the Squire at length became so obnoxious that violent hands were laid upon him and forced him to flee the country. It all happened in this manner. The patriots had erected a Liberty Pole, and at its top the Stars and Stripes waved defiance to all Tories. McFingal's blood was fired. Gathering his little band of retainers he attempted to cut down the unseemly staff. Naturally dire conflict ensued.

" At once with resolution fatal,
  Both Whigs and Tories rush'd to battle,
  Instead of weapons, either band
  Seized on such arms as came to hand.

        .   .   .   .   .   .

  So clubs and billets, staves and stones
  Met fierce, encountering every sconce,
  And cover'd o'er with knobs and pains
  Each void receptacle for brains.

        .   .   .   .   .   .

  And many a groan increas'd the din
  From batter'd nose and broken shin.
  McFingal, rising at the word,
  Drew forth his old militia-sword;
  Thrice cried ' King George,' as erst in distress,
  Knights of romance invoked a mistress;

        .   .   .   .   .   .

  And like a meteor rushing through,
  Struck on their Pole a vengeful blow.''

Affairs would have gone badly with the patriots

" Had not some Pow'r, a Whig at heart,
  Descended down and took their part
  (Whether 't were Pallas, Mars, or Iris,
  'Tis scarce worth while to make inquiries).''

This sympathetic Power, whoever he was,

urged a Whig to pick up a spade and advance
to the defence of the emblem of freedom. The
spade is mightier than the sword.

> " The sword perfidious fails its owner;
>   That sword, which oft had stood its ground,
>   By huge trainbands encircled round;
>   And on the bench, with blade right loyal,
>   Had won the day at many a trial,
>   Of stone and clubs had braved th' alarms,
>   Shrunk from these new Vulcanian arms.
>   The spade so temper'd from the sledge,
>   Nor keen nor solid harm'd its edge,
>   Now met it, from his arm of might,
>   Descending with steep force to smite;
>   The blade snapp'd short—and from his hand,
>   With rust embrown'd the glittering sand."

McFingal turns to call his friends.

> " In vain; the Tories all had run,
>   When scarce the fight was well begun:
>   Their setting wigs he saw decreas'd
>   Far in th' horizon tow'rd the west.
>
>   .   .   .   .   .   .
>
>   The fatal spade discharged a blow
>   Tremendous on his rear below."

The fate that now faces the Squire is indeed

a serious one. A court is hastily formed, and a decision still more hastily made.

> " Forthwith the crowd proceed to deck
> With halter'd noose McFingal's neck,
> While he in peril of his soul
> Stood tied half-hanging to the pole;
> Then lifting high the ponderous jar,
> Pour'd o'er his head the smoking tar.
>
> . . . .
>
> And now the feather-bag displayed
> Is waved in triumph o'er his head,
> And clouds him o'er with feathers missive,
> And down, upon the tar, adhesive:
> Not Maia's son, with wings for ears,
> Such plumage round his visage wore;
> Nor Milton's six wing'd angel gathers
> Such superfluity of feathers.
> Now all complete appears our Squire,
> Like Gorgon or Chimaera dire.''

Decked in this gay attire, McFingal sneaks away to his home, hides in a turnip bin in the cellar, and from this lowly station delivers a farewell address to the remnant of his frightened followers. Soon afterwards, he goes his way to Boston, hopeless and sick of Whigs and liberty.

There is a boisterous energy in all this, a

rude activity, that suited the not highly re-
fined but exceedingly earnest populace of the
day. Then, too, its satire is not so bitter but
that the very enemy himself might enjoy the
situations. One wonders if Irving was not unconsciously influenced by the once popular epic;
for the Knickerbocker History seems in not a
few pages a McFingal in prose. Moses Coit
Tyler, in his *Literary History of the American
Revolution,* calls the poem " one of the world's
masterpieces of political badinage,'' and such
praise is not extravagant. Though modelled
to some extent on Butler's *Hudibras,* it is undoubtedly much higher in tone, contains a
larger number of eloquent passages, and has in
general a more skilful polish than that famous
English classic. Here and there one seems to
hear snatches from the master-minds of ancient and modern days. And there is, in spite
of the subject and the treatment, a flavor of
culture through it all. And its author knew
all the tricks of the trade. It abounds in surprising rhymes, fantastic ideas, mock dignity,
and a jig-like movement which seldom fail to
excite merriment. Then, too, there is a Pope-
like talent for making memory-tempting coup-
lets. Who has not heard, for instance,

"No man e'er felt the halter draw,
With good opinion of the law "?

There has been from time to time some rather useless disputing among students of American literature as to whether Trumbull was influenced more by Butler or by the more bitter satirist, Churchill. It does not seem necessary to enter here into a discussion of the question. We know certainly that the story served its purpose and that it sounded through New England like a trumpet call. Everybody read it; everybody believed its truths; and everybody recognized its helpfulness. To us it presents in entertaining form an accurate portrayal of Revolutionary conditions and sentiments, just as it did to those strugglers before whom it placed in clearer light the ideals for which they were striving. For these reasons it gained the public ear, and, as far as may be expected of any piece of literature written for an emergency, still holds it. The poem is yet read, but its popularity should be greater; for aside from its historical interest and its power of entertaining, it shows the skilful use of a literary weapon which has been used in all the great struggles of the civilized world, and which will be used in the many to come.

I

Toward the close of the eighteenth century it happened that a number of Yale men were living in or near the town of Hartford, Connecticut. Now, whenever old students of one alma mater meet, they always feel like shouting the college song, giving the college yell, and closing the meeting with the singing of "Blest Be the Tie That Binds." Perhaps eighteenth century alumni were a trifle too dignified for that sort of thing; but they felt the bonds of college days nevertheless, and of course sometimes associated with one another until their little group really became a "club." Certainly the next most natural move in those days would be the reciting of original poems in these clubs, the reading of witty papers to one another, and finally debates on such timely subjects as Homer, Shakespeare, and "the great Mr. Pope." Now, you must remember that early newspapers were just as eager for good "copy" as the journals of to-day, and natu-

227

rally the third step in this club life would be the publication of the aforesaid poetic lines and witty essays.

THE HARTFORD WITS

In telling this, I have told you the story of the development of those Yale men into the once famous group known as the " Hartford Wits." Of course, there were other reasons for the group's existence. Yale men of that era, especially one, Timothy Dwight, who afterwards became president of Yale, considered Harvard men dangerously unorthodox. Indeed, some of those Harvard scholars boldly intimated that there wasn't an ounce of *brimstone* in all hell, while some of the younger fellows even had the audacity to doubt the very existence of that tropical settlement. Timothy Dwight, who was a clergyman of the original " blue-stocking " order, thought it was scandalous, and wrote in his *Triumph of Infidelity* some satirical lines about

" . . . the smooth Divine, unused to wound
The sinner's heart, with hell's alarming sound.
No terrors on his gentle tongue attend;
No grating truths the nicest ear offend."

Yale men thought it their sacred duty to combat Harvard in such a matter as this.

Then came far more important affairs. The Revolution was on, and the patriots needed every kind of aid possible. Nobly, even if at times somewhat crudely, the Hartford Wits responded. John Trumbull was one of them, and we know his part in the merciless ridicule of all that savored of Toryism; Timothy Dwight, who aided now and then, preached to the soldiers and wrote to the stay-at-homes; and, as we shall see later, nearly every other member of the little group, composed of such men as David Humphreys, M. F. Cogswell, Joel Barlow, Dr. Lemuel Hopkins, Theodore Dwight and Richard Alsop, served his country not only with pen but with arms. For a season war broke up the witty company, and they all could sympathize with one of the number who asked:

> " Amid the roar of drums and guns,
>   When meet again the Muses' sons ? "

But the struggle of arms past, " they hung up the sword in Hartford, and grasped the lyre." And the lyre must needs be a strong and often harsh one; for now many new dangers presented themselves and the times were indeed troubled. The war debt was thirty-eight millions; the lower classes refused to pay taxes; the paper money was almost worthless; the war veterans had not been paid for months; the bounties of land promised many of them had not been presented. Congress had promised the officers five years' extra pay, and the people objected loudly. The Cincinnati Society, founded by those who had been so fortunate or unfortunate as to wear shoulder-straps, was looked upon as an attempt to form a perpetual aristocracy in free America. France, in her wars, looked to the States for aid, and many hot-heads were in favor of granting it. Numerous mobs were formed in Connecticut, and a certain Shay had a miniature rebellion in Massachusetts. Participants in these lawless acts sought refuge in Rhode Island, and that " little but mighty " commonwealth refused to surrender them. Every State had its suspicions concerning a union, and preferred to be a republic by itself. The need of a centralized government was paramount. Some speaker of the day very cleverly said, " Thirteen staves and ne'er a hoop cannot make a

barrel.'' Many orators, however, were not so
reasonable, but, on the other hand, went about
the country making loud-mouthed appeals to
the people to rise in their might and sweep away,
the threatened monarchy.

Again, after the Union was more or less
firmly established, there were still other troubles. Those politicians who had opposed such
a close centralization became the Anti-Federalists or Democratic party, led by Thomas
Jefferson and Aaron Burr; while those who
took the opposite view formed the Federalists,
led by Washington, Hamilton, Madison, and
Jay. The Hartford Wits, for the most part,
had been and remained true to Washington,
and therefore to his party. Here indeed was
an opportunity for the display of peppery wit.
Then, too, those great events across the waters;
Napoleon and Nelson were before the eyes of
the world; a deadly conflict between monarchy
and democracy was on; and the Hartford Wits
felt called upon to encourage or discourage as
the spirit moved them. When all these topics
grew wearisome, there remained, of course, one
eternal subject—literary criticism. Then would
they take up the discussion of books and damn

authors and critics with an energy that would have put Dryden, Pope, and Byron to the blush. Even supposing that this theme grew tiresome, they could form a mutual admiration society and heartily praise one another.

For instance, one member wrote of another such lines as these:

" In lore of nations skilled, and brave in arms,
    See Humphreys glorious from the field retire,
    Sheathe the glad sword and string the tuneful lyre."

And another, Joel Barlow, author of the fearfully and wonderfully constructed *Columbiad* or *Vision of Columbus,* received this flattering notice:

" In Virgilian Barlow's tuneful lines
    With added splendor great Columbus shines."

What with rebuking Harvard sceptics, fighting in the field, ridiculing Tories, scolding taxpayers, opposing dishonest currency, condemning extravagant debts, encouraging the demands of soldiers, explaining the intentions of the Cincinnati Society, lashing mobs, discouraging State independence, supporting centralization, silencing " spread-eagle " orators, squelching fire-eating Jacobins, scourging Anti-

Federalists, commenting on foreign affairs, pooh-poohing critics, and praising one another, these Hartford Wits had about all they could well attend to. But, in all seriousness, they came in answer to a need of the struggling era, and Barrett Wendell is entirely correct when he says in his *History of Literature in America:* "An heroic, patriotic effort they stand for, and one made with enthusiasm, wit, and courage."

Undoubtedly they helped to an appreciable degree in the preservation of the nation. When it seemed that the petty jealousies of the separate colonies would effectually prevent a sound and permanent union, these writers in their serial poem, *The Anarchiad* (1786–7), placed before the people this all-important question:

" Shall lordly Hudson part contending powers,
 And broad Potomac lave two hostile shores?
 Must Alleghany's sacred summits bear
 The impious bulwarks of perpetual war,
 His hundred streams receive your heroes slain
 And bear your sons inglorious to the Main? "

It is evident that these wits were sometimes very serious. Note again some lines from *The Anarchiad* on that same momentous question: Shall we be one nation or many?

" Behold those veterans worn with want and care,
Their sinews stiffened, silvered o'er their hair,
Weak in their steps of age, they move forlorn,
Their toils forgotten by the sons of scorn;
This hateful truth still aggravates the pain,
In vain they conquered, and they bled in vain.

. . . .

For see, proud Faction waves her flaming brand,
And discord riots o'er the ungrateful land;

. . . .

In honor's seat the sons of meanness swarm,
And senates base the work of mobs perform,
To wealth, to power the sons of union rise,
While foes deride you and while friends despise.

. . . .

Go view the lands to lawless power a prey,
Where tyrants govern with unbounded sway;
See the long pomp in gorgeous state displayed,
The tinselled guards, the squadroned horse parade;

. . . .

High on the moving throne, and near the van,
The tyrant rides, the chosen scourge of man;
Clarions and flutes and drums his way prepare,
And shouting millions rend the conscious air;
Millions whose ceaseless toils the pomp sustain,
Whose hour of stupid joy repays an age of pain.

. . . .

Nor less abhorred the certain woe that waits
The giddy rage of democratic states;

. . . .

234

Led by wild demagogues the factious crowd,
Mean, fierce, imperious, insolent, and loud,
Nor fame nor wealth nor power nor system draws,
They see no object and perceive no cause,
But feel by turns, in one disastrous hour,
The extremes of license and the extremes of power.''

But this is not the sort of work in which they found the greatest delight or in which they most excelled. They enjoyed more thoroughly such exercise as Dwight's description of the mild and sweetly polite Harvard preacher mentioned above, or that description by Lemuel Hopkins of Thomas Jefferson, who posed as a pretty accurate scholar on everything from Anglo-Saxon to vaccination:

"Great sire of stories past belief;
Historian of the Mingo chief;
Philosopher of Indians' hair;
Inventor of a rocking-chair;
The correspondent of Mazze,
And Banneker less black than he!"

How they loved to poke fun at the versatile sage of Monticello! Upon taking the oath of office for the second time, March 4, 1805, Jefferson said in his inaugural address: "On taking this station on a former occasion, I de-

clared the principle on which I believed it my
duty to administer the affairs of our commonwealth. My conscience tells me that I have, on
every occasion, acted up to that declaration,
according to its obvious import and to the understanding of every candid mind.'' This was
indeed an opportunity for the men of Hartford,
and they grasped it while it was hot. Forthwith appeared a burlesque—the inaugural remarks of one, Jefferson:

" 'Tis just four years this all-eventful day,
  Since on my head devolved our country's sway.

          .   .   .   .

  You will remember with what modest air
  I first approached the Presidential Chair,
  How blushed my cheek, what faltering in my gait,
  When first I squatted on the throne of state!

          .   .   .   .

  A foolish custom forced me to declare
  Off-hand what point of compass I should steer;
  But knowing well that every Federal eye
  On me was fixed some mischief to descry,
  I tuned my fiddle for the vulgar throng,
  And lulled suspicion by a soothing song.''

He asked his conscience if he had broken the
promises of four years ago. Conscience answered that he had not.

" ' Thus, when you promised to be just and true
To *all* and give to every man his due,
Could Candor possibly have understood
That the term *all men* could your foes include?

. . . .

Nor shall the Federalists, perverse and base,
On grounds like these lay claim to hold their place.
Again, when toleration was your theme,
What stupid mortal could a moment dream
You meant to drop at once your choicest grace,
The right to turn the Federalists from place?

. . . .

Now, Sir, since I have set all matters right,
Conscience will bid the President good-night.' "

The effusions of the Hartford Wits may be
divided into three sections. The first series
of these satires and other poems, consisting in
all of twenty-four installments, was entitled
The Anarchiad, and dealt with the ruffian element in the lower classes and the subtle enemies
of union in the upper classes. These contributions, as well as some of those in the other
sections, were published in *The New Haven
Gazette,* and appeared in 1786 and 1787. Now,
you must know that these Yale men had considerable romance in their souls; therefore we
should not expect them to thrust these literary
efforts upon the world without some piquant

flavor of the wonderful and mysterious. No, indeed; it was solemnly stated that *The Anarchiad* had been dug up from the exceedingly ancient ruins of an Indian fort, where Madoc, a Welshman, who discovered America ages before Columbus had thought of being born, had buried the manuscript. It simply shows how surprisingly appropriate prophecies and advice intended for remote antiquity oftentimes are for the present moment; for these venerable hammerings of Madoc hit the eighteenth century nail squarely on the head. Anarch, the leader of the forces of confusion and ruin, which forces are, of course, the Anti-Federalists, urges all kinds of dangerous actions.

> " Stab Independence! dance o'er
> Freedom's grave! "

What else did these Democrats desire but the reign of confusion in the newly created nations?

> " The State surrounding with the wall of brass,
> And insurrections claim thy noblest praise,
> O'er Washington exact thy darling Shays,
> With thy contagion embryo mobs inspire,
> And blow to tenfold rage the kindling fire,
> Till the wide realm of discord bow the knee
> And hold true faith in Anarch and in thee."

The second section of the Hartford utterances was the series known as *The Echo,* the first poem of which appeared in the *American Mercury* of August, 1791, and the last in 1796. Written almost entirely by Richard Alsop and Theodore Dwight, a brother of Timothy, it mocked or " echoed " with multiplied reverberations the bombast and other exaggerations of the day. As the Duyckincks say in their *Cyclopædia of American Literature,* " If a penny-a-liner grew more maudlin and drunken in his style than usual; if an office-holder played his ' fantastic tricks,' a politician vapored, or a scientific pretender bored the public with his ignorance, or a French democratic procession moved at the heels of Genet, it was sure to be heard of from the banks of the Connecticut." From this more general purpose, however, the poem passed to the more specific and far more bitter one of ridiculing the Democrats on every possible occasion. We have seen how Jefferson and his inaugural address of 1805 were treated; the eccentric John Hancock, the rough and ready frontiersman Hugh Brackenridge, and many another Anti-Federalist, received just as merciless consideration.

" Leave us our Clinton, Jefferson and Co,
    These shall arouse us in the daily papers,
    And Jonny Hancock give us Negroe capers."

Every political move, no matter how honest its intention, was liable to attack; thus with Jay's Treaty:

" I say that we've determined, one and all,
    That Jay's vile treaty to the ground shall fall.
    Doubtless the subject will much heat excite,
    Blockheads will prate, and demagogues will write,
    From Club to Club the uproar will expand.
    .   .   .   .

    Full well I see how Democrats will meet,
    And drink seditious toasts at every treat,
    Roar out to liberty to save the land,
    And damn a treaty they don't understand."

Fear of the French and of their ultra-democratic notions was abroad in the land, and such lines as the following, known to have been written by Lemuel Hopkins, must have gained the applause of all good Federalists:

" See fraught with democratic lore,
    Genet arriv'd on Charleston shore.
    But, as was meet, first broach'd his mission
    To men of sans-culotte condition;
    Who thronged around with open throats,
    As round old Crusoe flock'd the goats,

And learn'd his sermon, to his wishes,
As Austin taught huge shoals of fishes;
Made all the anti-federal presses
Screech shrill hosannas, styl'd addresses;
And while to Court he took his way
Sung hallelujahs to Genet;

．　．　．　．　．　．　．　．　．

Like Hessian flies, import'd o'er,
Clubs self-create infest our shore."

As we have noted, however, these satires
were not intended solely for political purposes.
Anything extravagant was a sufficient incentive for a sarcastic broadside. For instance,
it seems that a Boston newspaper attempted in
July, 1791, to give a poetic description of a
storm occurring there, and the result was a
poetic " echo," from which the following lines
are taken:

" On Tuesday last great Sol, with piercing eye,
Pursued his journey thro' the vaulted sky,
And in his car effulgent roll'd his way
Four hours beyond the burning zone of day;
When lo! a cloud, o'er shadowing all the plain,
From countless pores perspir'd a *liquid* rain,
While from its cracks the lightnings made a peep,
And chit-chat thunders rock'd our fears asleep.
But soon the vapory fog dispersed in air,
And left the azure blue-eyed concave bare;

Even the last drop of hope, which dripping skies
Gave for a moment to our straining eyes,
Like *Boston Rum*, from heaven's *junk bottles* broke,
Lost all the corks, and vanished into smoke.
But swift, from worlds unknown, a fresh supply
Of vapor dimm'd the great horizon's eye;

. . . .

The seen and unseen worlds grew dark, and nature
    'gan to weep.

. . . .

Majestic thunders, with disploding roar,
And sudden crashing, bounced along the shore,
Till, lost in other lands, the whispering sound
Fled from our ears and fainted on the ground.

. . . .

N.B. At Cambridge town, the self-same day,
A barn was burnt well-fill'd with hay.
Some say the lightning turned it red,
Some say the thunder struck it dead,
Some say it made the cattle stare,
And some it kill'd an aged mare;
But we expect the truth to learn
From Mr. Wythe, who own'd the barn.''

The third section of the Hartford serial tirade was entitled *The Political Green House,* and appeared in 1799. It is for the most part a review of the previous year, and uses the various important events of those twelve months as a means of attacking Jefferson and all Jacobins. Here, too, is found an attack upon one of their own Wits, Joel Barlow, who is accused of stealing parts of the *Anarchiad* for his *Conspiracy of Kings*. As Barlow had written no small part of the *Anarchiad,* doubtless he thought he might borrow his own; but the *Green House* writer, probably Alsop, declares it " a prominent trait of the Jacobinical character to take what belongs to others, without leave and without paying for it." All measures against the French receive hearty praise; the Alien and Sedition Law is a joy forever; while Vermont, in running all the Jacobins out of office, has become an earthly Paradise.

Now, in 1807, *The Echo* and *The Political Green House,* with a poem entitled *A Poetico-Political Olio, consisting of extracts from Democracy, an Epic Poem,* were published as one volume with the title, *The Echo with Other Poems.* (The " general reader " may, of course, skip all such dry facts and dates if he finds them uninteresting; they are intended for those unfortunates who occupy college chairs of literature and who must gather vast masses

of minute details in order to astonish their awe-
stricken students.) But to resume: *The Echo*
and *The Political Green House* thus printed together enjoyed considerable vogue long after
the disturbances that created them had been
forever settled; and doubtless this later entertainment was more whole-souled than in the
old days when Anti-Federalists, reading these
roughly printed sheets, found themselves handled without gloves.

But all America knows that those Federalists fought a losing battle and that the Democrats, with Jefferson as leader, turned the tide
of the American political sea. And it seems
that the Hartford Wits also knew it; for toward
the last the satire was not so stinging as in
earlier days, the laughter was not so whole-
hearted, and now and again the poets seemed
to be asking themselves, '' How will the people
take this? '' Like most mortals, they at length
began to have opposing opinions, grew discouraged or uninterested, and gave it up; and thus
the Hartford Wits, *as a body*, died a natural
death. But, as *individuals*, they were rather
lively corpses for some years after their fra-
ternity or club had been interred.

II

And now, of course the most natural question in the world at this juncture would be, " Who were these wits as individuals? " In the last quarter of the eighteenth century Hartford and New Haven had some very brilliant citizens, and the " Wits " were the cream of the milk. Originally this fine fellowship or junto consisted of probably only four members, Timothy Dwight, John Trumbull, David Humphreys, and Joel Barlow; but toward the close of the war days such men entered the circle as Dr. Lemuel Hopkins, Richard Alsop, and Theodore Dwight, and these, with occasional aid from two or three other citizens of Connecticut, made things lively. Here Wordsworth might have written another " We are Seven; " he could not have selected seven more active, brainy, and versatile characters in all America. Let us glance at the varied and useful lives of them all, and, at the same time, as we have seen what they could do as a whole, let us see what each could do as an individual writer.

TIMOTHY DWIGHT

Timothy Dwight has small right to appear in this or any other book of humor; and he is mentioned here with the Wits mainly because in his younger days he wrote lines against Harvard sinfulness, and encouraged and sometimes aided these verse-writers dwelling in or near Hartford town. His humorous verse, however, was very meagre, and should always have been labelled clearly. His forte lay in producing an epic containing nine thousand, six hundred and seventy-two never read lines entitled *The Conquest of Canaan*. Another poem of his, *Greenfield Hill*, is shorter and therefore no worse. Then, too, every school-boy knows that he wrote the once admired *Ode to Columbia,* beginning,

" Columbia, Columbia, to glory arise! "

but no school-boy wades through it unless a merciless teacher condemns him to the ordeal. As we all know, Dr. Dwight at length became president of Yale, preached many solemn and elongated sermons, and at last, full of years, honors, and theology, returned unto his fathers.

DAVID HUMPHREYS

John Trumbull we have already discussed. It is not difficult to discern the flavor of his satire throughout *The Anarchiad* and the other works of the group; for now and then one comes across lines that could have dropped from no other pen of the day. A man who was often at his side, and who with him penned many a sharp verse, was Colonel David Humphreys (1753-1818), soldier, diplomatist, wit, and genial gentleman. His was a life lived to the brim. Born at Derby, Connecticut, he graduated at Yale, entered the Revolutionary Army as a captain, and served from 1780 until the close of the strife as aide-de-camp to Washington. The friendship that existed between the wit and the great general became a tie that bound them closely until death. For months at a time Humphreys lived at Mt. Vernon, and he and Washington always acted like brothers. That he was a brave warrior is shown by the fact that Congress presented him with a sword for gallantry at Yorktown; and that he was a firm believer in the rights of the struggling people is evidenced by his *Address to the Armies of the United States* (1782)—which, by the way, you will be spared here, as its length is one of its most conspicuous characteristics.

After his service in the army, he held the important position of secretary of the legation —Jefferson, Franklin, and Adams—at Paris, and while thus employed wrote another widely noticed poem—a thousand lines this time—on the " Happiness of America." It contains some well turned verses, as may be seen from the following:

" There some old warrior, grown a village sage,
Whose locks are whitened with the frosts of age,
While life's low-burning lamp renews its light,
With tales heroic shall beguile the night;
Shall tell of battles fought, of feats achieved,
And sufferings ne'er by human heart conceived

. . . .

Troops strive with troops; ranks, bending, press on
    ranks;
O'er slippery plains the struggling legions reel;
Then livid lead and Burgoyne's glittering steel
With dark-red wounds their mangled bosoms bore;
While furious coursers, snorting foam and gore,
Bear wild their riders o'er the carnaged plain,
And, falling, roll them headlong on the slain.

. . . .

Thus will the veteran tell the tale of wars,
Disclose his breast, to count his glorious scars;
In mute amazement hold the listening swains;
Make freezing horror creep through all their veins;
Or oft, at freedom's name, their souls inspire
With patriot ardor and heroic fire.''

In those days ability to write meant advancement in the political world, and consequently in 1786 we see Humphreys a member of the State Legislature. Soon, however, he was back at Mt. Vernon, translating de Mièrre's *The Widow of Malabar,* to be acted by Hallam's American Company at Philadelphia in 1790. In 1794 he became our first ambassador to Lisbon; in 1797 he was made minister to Spain; and in 1802 he returned to America, and henceforth devoted much of his time to introducing merino sheep into the New World. He became decidedly interested in this sheep industry, and even wrote a poem about it, in the course of which he says:

'' Oh, might my guidance from the downs of Spain
Lead a white flock across the western main;
Fam'd like the bark that bore the Argonaut
Should be the vessel with the burden fraught!
Clad in the raiment my Merinos yield,
Like Cincinnatus fed from my own field;
Far from ambition, grandeur, care, and strife,

In sweet fruition of domestic life;
There would I pass with friends beneath my trees,
What rests from public life; in letter'd ease."

Although sixty years old when the War of 1812 began, he entered the army as a brigadier-general, and served throughout the campaign. Thus his days until his death at New Haven six years later were full of activity and reward.

Humphreys was not a strikingly original man; but he had energy and perseverance, and he could polish a line or add a sharp word or two to the pointed verses of his colleagues. It would not be of special interest to try to point out just what Humphreys did or did not write in the various poems of the Hartford Wits. Perhaps, after all, it could not be done. But, if you would see a specimen of his individual wit, here are some lines from *The Monkey,* " who shaved himself and his friends."

" A man who own'd a barber's shop
   At York, and shaved full many a fop,
A monkey kept for his amusement;
   He made no other kind of use on't—

   .   .   .   .

" It chanc'd in shop, the dog and cat,
   While friseur din'd, demurely sat,

Jacko found naught to play the knave in,
So thought he'd try his hand at shaving.
Around the shop in haste he rushes,
And gets the razors, soap, and brushes;
Now puss he fix'd (no muscle stirs)
And lather'd well her beard and whiskers,
Then gave a gash, as he began—
The cat cry'd ' waugh! ' and off she ran.

" Next Towser's beard he tried his skill in,
Though Towser seemed somewhat unwilling:
As badly here again succeeding,
The dog runs howling round, and bleeding.

" Nor yet was tir'd our roguish elf;
He'd seen the barber shave himself;
So by the glass upon the table,
He rubs with soap his visage sable,
Then with left hand holds smooth his jaw,—
The razor in his dexter paw;
Around he flourishes and slashes,
Till all his face is seam'd with gashes.
His cheeks dispatch'd—his visage thin
He cock'd, to shave beneath his chin;
Drew razor swift as he could pull it,
And cut, from ear to ear, his gullet.

Moral
" Who cannot write, yet handle pens,
Are apt to hurt themselves and friends.
Though others use them well, yet fools
Should never meddle with edge tools."

III

JOEL BARLOW

Of all the Hartford Wits, excluding John Trumbull, doubtless the best known in our day is Joel Barlow (1754-1812). Who has not read his *Hasty Pudding?*

> "I sing the sweets I know, the charms I feel,
> My morning incense and my evening meal,
> The sweets of Hasty Pudding."

It is interesting to see what a poetic product he could make out of such a subject as "mush" and out of many other subjects no less prosaic; but his life, it would seem, is far more interesting than anything he wrote. How manifold were his activities, how romantic his adventures, and how miserable his end! He was born at Reading, Connecticut, and was educated at Dartmouth and at Yale. When he received his B.A. from the latter college in 1778, he read as the class-poem, *The Prospect of Peace,* verses full of patriotism and unusual benevolence toward all nations. In 1781 he received the M.A. from his alma mater. But during his vacations Barlow had spent his leisure time fighting the British, and the taste of army life thus experienced so pleased him that he studied theology six weeks and entered the ranks as a chaplain some months before receiving the master's degree. After the Revolution he studied law and was admitted to the bar at Hartford in 1785. During that same year he was given the task of revising Watts' version of the Psalms, and did it very acceptably, although some caustic wit of the day exclaimed:

" You've proved yourself a sinful cre'tur;
  You've murdered Watts and spoilt the meter;
  You've tried the word of God to alter,
  And for your pains deserve a halter."

At Hartford Barlow founded *The American Mercury*, in which *The Echo* and other poems by the Wits appeared; and there, too, in 1787 he published his loud-sounding, but rather tiresome *Vision of Columbus*. This vision embraces Heaven, Earth, and Hell, and all that lie therein, and was considered in its day a marvellous accomplishment. The verses brought him fame, and before long he was appointed European agent of the Scioto Land

Company. He opened an office in Paris, advertised lavishly, and sent broadcast among the people this glowing description of the Ohio valley, where the company's lands were located: "Farms for sale on the banks of the Ohio, *la belle rivière;* the finest district of the United States! Healthful and delightful of climate; scarcely any frost in winter; fertile soil; a boundless inland navigation; magnificent forests of a tree from which sugar flows; excellent fishing and fowling; venison in abundance; no wolves, lions, or tigers; no taxes; no military duty. All these unexampled advantages offered to colonists at five shillings the acre!"

This sounds rather modern, does it not? The company, too, was modern; it proved to be a fake of the first water, and Barlow, besieged by the butcher, the baker, and the candlestick maker, all of whom wanted their money back, was glad to resign his position and look for other fields of labor. He was not long in the seeking. The French Revolution was drawing near; the French people were full of excitement, and Barlow felt called upon to enter Parisian politics. Having translated Volney's

Ruins, he took it over to London for publication, and while there wrote his violent *Advice to the Privileged Classes,* a work which was promptly proscribed by the British government. Not content with this, he composed *The Conspiracy of Kings* against the enemies of France, and aroused still more bitterness. He became a member of the Constitution Society, was sent as a British delegate to the French Convention, and received as a parting gift a present of one thousand pairs of shoes. It was at this time, it is thought, that he wrote his *Song to the Guillotine:*

> " Fame, let thy trumpet sound,
> Tell all the world around—
>   How Capet fell;
> And when great George's poll
> Shall in the basket roll,
> Let mercy then control
>   The Guillotine.

> " When all the sceptred crew
> Have paid their homage to
>   The Guillotine;
> Let freedom's flag advance,
> Till all the world, like France!
> O'er tyrants' graves shall dance,
>   And peace begin."

In Paris he became a speculator, gained great wealth, lived like a king, and widened the sphere of his political power. His country, recognizing his diplomatic qualities, chose him as consul to Algiers from 1795 to 1797, and there he rendered valuable service in liberating American prisoners and making with the neighboring petty powers treaties then considered advantageous but now looked upon as disgraceful.

By 1805 Barlow had returned to America. Jefferson received him with open arms; he was hailed as a shrewd diplomat; and his verses convinced the people that he was no less a poet. His immense and unwieldly *Columbiad* and his *Hasty Pudding,* the latter prepared during his active work in France, found a multitude of readers. His affairs were indeed prosperous. Having built a splendid home in Washington, he hovered about the powers that were, with the result that in 1811 he was appointed minister to France. Now came the closing scene. Napoleon requested a conference with him at Wilna; then occurred the retreat from Moscow; and Barlow, necessarily involved in it, followed the army until one evening in a little Polish village his strength failed him and he died in wretchedness. How bitterly he felt the disaster and how scornfully he regarded Napoleon we may judge from his last poem, dictated as he lay on his death-bed in that bleak, starving, snow-covered town:

Advice to a Raven in Russia.

" Black fool, why winter here? These frozen skies,
Worn by your wings and deafened by your cries,
Should warn you hence, where milder suns invite,
And Day alternates with his mother Night.
You fear, perhaps, your food will fail you there—
Your human carnage, that delicious fare,
That lured you hither, following still your friend,
The great Napoleon, to the world's bleak end.

.   .   .   .

You fear he left behind no wars to feed
His feather'd cannibals and nurse the breed.
Fear not, my screamer, call your greedy train,
Sweep over Europe, hurry back to Spain—
You'll find his legions there, the valiant crew
Please best their master when they toil for you.

.   .   .   .

Choose then your climate, fix your best abode—
He'll make you deserts, he'll bring you blood.

.   .   .   .

War after war his hungry soul requires;
State after state shall sink beneath his fires.

.   .   .   .

Till men resume their souls, and dare to shed
Earth's total vengeance on the monster's head!''

It was while in Paris in 1793, so some of the
accounts say, that Barlow wrote his yet famous
Hasty Pudding; but it was not until 1796 that
it was presented to American readers through
the columns of a New Haven paper. Far from
home, he began to think of the plain, old-fash-
ioned New England food, and memory brought
back even the minute details of it all. See the
note he appended to the poem; French cooks
and French etiquette had not destroyed his native simplicity; '' There are various ways of
preparing and eating it; with molasses, butter,
sugar, cream, and fried. Why so excellent a
thing cannot be eaten alone? Nothing is perfect alone, even man, who boasts of so much perfection, is nothing without his fellow substance.
In eating, beware of the lurking heat that lies
deep in the mass; dip your spoon gently, take
shallow dips, and cool it by degrees. It is
sometimes necessary to blow. This is indicated
by certain signs which every experienced feeder
knows. They should be taught to young begin-
ners. I have known a child's tongue blistered
for want of this attention, and then the school-

dame would insist that the poor thing had told a lie. . . . A prudent mother will cool it for her child with her own sweet breath. The husband, seeing this, pretends his own wants blowing too from the same lips. A sly deceit of love. She knows the cheat, but feigning ignorance, lends her pouting lips and gives a gentle blast, which warms the husband's heart more than it cools the pudding.''

The poem itself is in three stately cantos, with here an echo of Dryden and there an echo of Pope,—very distant echoes, however, it must be admitted. And yet, the mock heroic strain is well sustained throughout. The old saying goes thus: '' The proof of the pudding is the eating of it; '' therefore, test for yourself the flavor of *Hasty Pudding:*

'' Oh! could the smooth, the emblematic song
   Flow like thy genial juices o'er my tongue,
   Could those mild morsels in my numbers chime,
   And, as they roll in substance, roll in rhyme,
   No more thy awkward unpoetic name
   Should shun the muse or prejudice thy fame;
   But rising grateful to the accustom'd ear,
   All bards should catch it, and all realms revere!

    • • • • • • • • •

Dear Hasty Pudding, what unpromised joy
Expands my heart, to meet thee in Savoy!
Doom'd o'er the world through devious paths to
    roam,
Each clime my country and each house my home,
My soul is soothed, my cares have found an end,
I greet my long lost, unforgotten friend.
For thee through Paris, that corrupted town,
How long in vain I wandered up and down,
Where shameless Bacchus, with his drenching hoard,
Cold from his cave usurps the morning board.
London is lost in smoke and steep'd in tea;
No Yankee there can lisp the name of thee;
The uncouth word, a libel on the town,
Would call a proclamation from the crown."

And see what results come from a hasty pudding diet. Barlow recognizes the pleasant and useful qualities of other items in the vegetable kingdom; but, after all, what can compare with corn?

" My song resounding in its grateful glee,
No merit claims: I praise myself in thee.
My father loved thee through his length of days!
For thee his fields were shaded o'er with maize;
From thee what health, what vigor he possess'd,
Ten sturdy freemen from his loins attest;
Thy constellation ruled my natal morn,
And all my bones were made of Indian corn."

The simplicity of New England life, he declares, has been the salvation of the nation; and Hasty Pudding is the symbol of that simplicity.

" To mix the food by vicious rules of art,
  To kill the stomach, and to sink the heart,
  To make mankind to social virtue sour,
  Cram o'er each dish, and be what they devour;
  For this the kitchen muse first fram'd her book,
  Commanding sweats to stream from every cook;
  Children no more their antic gambols tried,
  And friends to physic wonder'd why they died.
  Not so the Yankee—his abundant feast,
  With simples furnish'd and with plainness drest,
  A numerous offspring gathers round the board,
  And cheers alike the servant and the lord;
  Whose well-bought hunger prompts the joyous taste,
  And health attends them from the short repast."

Here, then, is an embryo *Snowbound* or *Cotter's Saturday Night*,—rude, but energetic, with true though humble descriptions, and a quiet humor that makes the poem throughout a decidedly pleasant piece of reading. Barlow's sarcastic lines on Englishmen and Tories were undoubtedly an aid to the American cause; but not by these will the future remember him. *Hasty Pudding* alone will keep his memory green; for it is

"A name, a sound to every Yankee dear."

261

IV

RICHARD ALSOP

Of the other leading spirits among the Wits, by far the most enthusiastic was Richard Alsop (1761-1815). In fact, Alsop was, after a time, the very genius and life of the endeavor. A versatile fellow, acquainted with the literature of several languages, fond of outdoor life, something of a naturalist, quick and varied in conversation, fond of every phase of life, he was a person of interest to all kinds and conditions of men.

He early became interested in the efforts of his fellow Yale graduates, helped write the first number of *The Echo* in 1791, and was busy in this sort of " well doing " until its close in 1805. His *Poem: Sacred to the Memory of George Washington* (1809) was widely read, while a number of translations added to his fame,—especially his *Enchanted Lake of the Fairy Morgana* (1806), which, we are informed,

was a translation from the *Orlando Inamorato*
of Francesco Berni. Of course, the " gentle
reader " is acquainted with this classic, and I
shall therefore not dwell upon its merits. Besides, I have not read it, and might make some
misleading statements. I might discuss, also,
his *Charms of Fancy;* but as it extends through
five books, doubtless the reader will be charmed
to have it left to his own fancy.

In spite, however, of these weighty efforts to
write masterpieces, Richard Alsop was a natural wit,—a genial humorist who, like Irving,
poked a gentle sort of fun at the follies of his
day. Perhaps, if it had been possible, he
would have preferred to make his witticisms
without touching anybody's tender spots; for
he possessed a talent for creating humor for its
own sake, a humor that both friend and foe
could enjoy. The *Newspaper Thunder Storm,*
quoted in previous pages, was from his pen,
and, while sarcastic, there is in it nothing of
the offensive tone so frequently found in the
satires of his era. But, because Alsop preferred genial humor, we must not think him
unable to fence with the sharp blade of wit. In
the course of a century or two, the Puritanism

of New England had begun to thaw into a rather cool but nevertheless acceptable liberalism; and the followers of Shakespeare and Ben Jonson, always on the lookout for a good opening, quietly entered the land of the Blue Laws, and ventured to give barn-storming theatrical exhibitions under the pseudonym of "moral lectures." Governor Hancock was noted for his vinegar-flavored piety, and we should not be surprised therefore to learn that he sent the Massachusetts Assembly a message calling attention to the fact that "Stage plays, Interludes, and Theatrical Entertainments under the style and appellation of 'Moral Lectures'" were being presented in the State, directly in defiance of the ancient laws of the Commonwealth. This was on November 8, 1792. On November 10 Alsop published in *The Echo* a long and witty parody on the paper. Perhaps some extracts will give you a better idea of the poem and of the poet than any further words on my part.

" A thing most vile, most dreadful in its kind,
　　Hangs, like a mill-stone, heavy on my mind;
　　By conscience urged, in duty's cause made bold,
　　To you this wicked thing I shall unfold,

Since plain enough to *me* is its intent,
An open insult on *my* government.
Long since, while Britain with maternal hand,
Cheer'd the lov'd offspring of Columbia's land,

. . . .

This State, then Province, pass'd with wise intent,
An Act, *Stage-Plays* and such things to prevent:
You'll find it, sirs, among the Laws sky blue,
Made near that time on brooms when Witches flew.

. . . .

Yet, notwithstanding this, some chaps uncivil,
Grand emissaries of our foe the Devil,
Aliens and *Foreigners* and *Actors* funny,
Who less esteem our morals than our money;
Even in *our* holy Capital of late,
Have dared insult the majesty of state,
And to exhibit publicly, propose,
Stage-Plays and *Interludes* and *Heathen Shows;*
Which in the garb of *Moral Lectures* drest,
Of our good, sober manners make a jest.

. . . .

Judge, Gentlemen! *my* feelings when at first
This information on my ear-drum burst:
Not more was Israel's hapless King appall'd
When Endor's witch the ghost of Samuel call'd.

. . . .

Wild consternation on my visage hung,
Congeal'd my blood, and every nerve unstrung;

O'er my whole frame a palsying horror flew,
And *sense,* retiring, bade a long adieu.

. . . .

With joy extreme, O gentlemen! in you
The firm upholders of the laws I view,
On you devolves the task (I grant it great),
To keep unstain'd the chasteness of our *State:*
Since that *good lady* is beset so sore
By rakes and libertines full many a score.

. . . .

And whate'er punishment you shall devise,
As to your noble judgments seemeth wise;
Whether you burn, drown, knock them on the head,
Or hang them by the neck till dead, dead, dead—

. . . .

I hope a great example it will stand,
And *in terrorem* guard *our* pious land."

V

LEMUEL HOPKINS

The work done by Theodore Dwight consisted mainly of suggesting a line here and there, and of sharpening the points of some of the satires produced by the others; but the work done by Dr. Lemuel Hopkins (1750-1801) was much more definite and shows individuality if not positive talent. Hopkins was an eccentric physician, long-legged and staring-eyed, and yet a man skilled in his profession and strikingly intelligent. Long after his death the story continued to be told of his having found a child suffering with scarlet fever lying in a closed room and covered with a multitude of blankets, and of how he seized it and ran, wild-eyed, from the house. The family, thinking him demented, pursued him with brooms, pokers, rolling pins, anything at hand. Hopkins, however, hurried to a tree nearby, placed the child under the cool shade, calmly asked for some wine for the little one, and soon had the child delivered from its delirium. And yet, splendid physician as he was, he lived in constant fear of consumption, and had himself bled so often that he did indeed at last die from a lung trouble brought on by this weakening surgery.

In spite of his strange manners, Hopkins was sound of heart and stood boldly for what he believed. When General Ethan Allen wrote a work upholding infidelity, the sharp-witted doctor came back at him with a poem—a mighty weapon in a skilful hand.

" Lo, Allen 'scaped from British jails,
   His tushes broke by biting nails,
   Appears in Hyperborean skies,
   To tell the world the Bible lies.
   See him on green hills north afar
   Glow like a self-enkindled star,
   Prepar'd (with mob-collecting club
   Black from the forge of Belzebub,
   And grin with metaphysic scowl,
   With quill just plucked from wing of owl)
   As rage or reason rise or sink,
   To shed his blood, or shed his ink.
   Behold inspired from Vermont dens
   The seer of Antichrist descends,
   To feed new mobs with Hell-born manna
   In Gentile lands of Susquehanna;

And teach the Pennsylvania Quaker
High blasphemies against his maker.

. . . .

All front he seems like wall of brass,
And brays tremendous as an ass;
One hand is clench'd to batter noses,
While t'other scrawls 'gainst Paul and Moses."

We know, too, that he wrote some of the bitter lines against Jefferson, already quoted, and parts of that strong plea to the States, also quoted above, beginning with the words:

"Go view the lands to lawless power a prey."

He had no patience whatever with the many quacks whom the lax medical laws of the day allowed to prey upon the people, and some of his bitterest expressions are against these vampires. For many years a popular poem at the New England fire-side was his *Victim of the Cancer Quack:*

" Here lies a fool flat on his back,
The victim of a cancer quack;
Who lost his money and his life,
By plaster, caustic, and by knife.
The case was this—A pimple rose
South-east a little of his nose,

269

Which daily reddened and grew bigger,
As too much drinking gave it vigor.
A score of gossips soon ensure
Full threescore different modes of cure;
But yet the full-fed pimple still
Defied all petticoated skill;
When fortune led him to peruse
A hand-bill in the weekly news,
Signed by six fools of different sorts,
All cured of cancers made of warts,
Who recommend, with due submission,
This cancer-monger as magician.

. . . .

The bargain struck, the plaster on,
Which gnawed the cancer at its leisure,
And pained his face above all measure.
But still the pimple spread the faster,
And swelled like toad that meets disaster.

. . . .

Then purged him pale with jalap drastic,
And next applied the infernal caustic.
But yet, this semblance bright of hell
Served but to make the patient yell;
And, gnawing on with fiery pace,
Devoured one broadside of his face.
' Courage 'tis done,' the doctor cried,
And quick the incision knife applied:
That with three cuts made such a hole
Out flew the patient's tortured soul! ''

These, then, were the leaders of the little
group of wits who made many a politician and
impostor of colonial days writhe under the well-
knotted lash. Much that they wrote was the
veriest doggerel, and some of them knew it;
but whatever they produced was wildly applauded by their friends and dreaded by their
enemies. It was a unique movement in those
old days, and its success was unequalled by like
attempts until a similar organization known as
the Croaker Poets arose years later in New
York City. Those broadsides—*The Anarchiad,
The Echo, The Political Green House,* and
others—fulfilled a positive need of the times,
and no matter how indifferent their literary
qualities, their importance in the making of the
nation is worthy of no small consideration.

VI

HUGH BRACKENRIDGE

Now, we must not think that the victims of these Hartford Wits aimed no arrows in reply; several of the persecuted returned hot missives. The Wits had at least one notable and worthy opponent—Hugh Brackenridge (1748-1816). Brackenridge was a " furious " Democrat, a man so violent in his oppositions that, according to his son's testimony, he resigned a position as judge for fear he should, while holding office, inflict bodily injury upon a political enemy. And yet, strange as it may seem, we have to-day scarcely a scrap of his satirical comments upon the Federalists. His son states that the father was exceedingly careless about his manuscripts, considering them worthless as soon as they had served their purpose; and doubtless it is because of this characteristic that his fame as a brilliant political wit rests mainly on tradition. He left to posterity, however, one work which bears the marks of genius:—the Duyckincks speak of it as one of the greatest political satires yet produced in America. That work is *Modern Chivalry, or the Adventures of Captain Farrago and Teague O'Regan, His Servant* (1796–1806). Brackenridge, the early follower of Jefferson and erstwhile staunch admirer of the " common people," had so changed his views under a decade or two of Democratic government that now he had almost lost faith in the genius of the populace for self-rule. If you are a believer in the infallibility of Democracy, read this book, and your faith will be considerably shaken.

Brackenridge's life, like that of nearly every other humorist whom we have discussed, was full of activity. Born in Scotland, he came at the age of five with his parents and their numerous other children, to America. The father was so poverty-stricken that upon landing he had to sell his only coat to buy the family some food, and it is known that all walked nearly the entire distance from New York City to York County, Pennsylvania. There they leased a backwoods farm and nearly starved to death before the first crop came. But who ever heard of a Scotchman's failing? Hugh Brackenridge not only survived the lack of food and the unremitting toil, but at the same time learned Latin and Greek from a circuit-riding parson, " swapped " his knowledge of these for lessons in mathematics, and at fifteen was ready to teach school. Those were days of arduous struggle for the boy; often he walked thirty miles to obtain a book and then spent the night reading it by the light of a log-fire. That at the age of fifteen he was well prepared to teach the old-time country-school every one may judge for himself. He went down to Gunpowder Falls, Maryland, to instruct, found among the students a giant bully who had thrashed all former teachers, and, having tried persuasion in vain, " seized a brand from the fire, knocked the rebel down, and spread terror around him." From that day the discipline at Gunpowder Falls was exemplary.

But Brackenridge would never have been content as a mere country school-teacher. Soon he was at Princeton, serving as a tutor and general utility man, and studying with the same zest as in his boyhood. When he graduated in 1771, he recited with Freneau a dialogue,

The Rising Glory of America,—a poem which, as we have seen, was widely read throughout the colonies. He still remained at Princeton several months, tutoring and studying theology, and then, after receiving license to preach, he returned to Maryland, where he preached and supervised a highly successful academy.

It was while he was thus engaged that the Battle of Bunker Hill occurred. The strain was too much for his Scotch blood. He hastily prepared a vigorous drama entitled *Bunker Hill,* which was published a few months later, and during the same year, 1776, hurried away to Philadelphia. There he edited the *United States Magazine*, a journal that did good service in lashing the Tories and other foes of the new government, and in it he did work that gained him wide notoriety and not a few bitter enemies. Having written one day a severe stricture on General Lee's conduct toward Washington, he was called upon the next morning by the fiery general to receive a thrashing. In response to an earthquake of a knock, Brackenridge stuck his head out an upstairs window, whereupon Lee shook his fist at him and shouted,

275

" Come down, and I'll give you as good a horse-whipping as any rascal ever received! "

" Excuse me, general," calmly replied Brackenridge; " but I wouldn't come down for two such favors! "

Soon we find Brackenridge serving as a chaplain in the Continental Army. What fiery sermons were his! Six of them were published in 1778 under the title, *Six Political Discourses Founded on the Scripture;* the publisher did a very dangerous thing not to print them on asbestos! How Brackenridge could hate! Listen to a few Christian remarks concerning the British: " Let every class of men join to execrate the tyrant and the tyranny, and to rank the George of England with the Cains and the murderers of mankind. Let fathers teach their sons the degenerate nature and the name of Englishmen—let mothers still with this the children on the breast, and make the name a bugbear. . . . Let every man become a soldier. . . . Let him be of the mind to fight from hill to hill, from vale to vale, and on every plain, until the enemy is driven back, and forced to depart,—until the tyrant shall give up his claim, and be obliged to confess that free men, that Americans, are not to be subdued."

Now, Brackenridge never did like preaching, so he said; and, moreover, he had his serious doubts as to the veracity of Presbyterian doctrines. He turned to the law, studied in the office of Samuel Chase at Annapolis, and in 1781 went to Pittsburgh, then a small village, and was almost immediately chosen for the State Legislature. Now came the trouble over the tax on liquor, and Brackenridge, with characteristic impetuosity, was so bitterly opposed to the excise that he aided in the Whiskey Insurrection in Pennsylvania, and was obliged to defend himself in 1795 by publishing his *Incidents of the Insurrection in the Western Part of Pennsylvania.*

All this was but an unconscious preparation for his masterpiece, *Modern Chivalry;* for some of the most laughable portions of the book deal with these very matters of excise and rebellion. The first part of the work appeared in 1796, and ten years later came the second part. The book became almost a household classic in the western territory. One day, while at a frontier inn, Brackenridge asked the landlord if he had anything to read. " That I have," said the host, as he reached down under the bar and pulled out *Modern Chivalry.* " There is something will make you laugh, and the man that wrote it was no fool neither.'' Years afterward a descendant of the author, while travelling through Mississippi, was asked whether he was related to the Brackenridge who wrote *Modern Chivalry,* and, upon stating that he was, immediately was offered a horse by the native, and could persuade the owner to take no pay for its use.

We should not be surprised, therefore, to find Brackenridge succeeding from this time forth. In 1799 he was appointed Judge of the Supreme Court of Pennsylvania, a position which he honored by his unswerving integrity until his death in 1816. And yet, in spite of his dignified office, he was always full of wit, and is said to have found but one man whom he could not make laugh immediately. That man was George Washington. One evening at a social meeting he tried all his powers upon the Father of the Country; but not one smile flitted across the sombre face. That night, however, Brackenridge had his revenge. Lying in a room adjoining Washington's, he heard the general giggling far into the night. It is not known whether George of the Hatchet was slow to see a joke or whether he discovered Brackenridge's intention and determined not to be overcome in the presence of the other guests.

Modern Chivalry is rough in its flavor, not always delicate in its expression, but ever positive and manly in its sentiments. One finds in it here and there reminders of old Don Quixote. Captain Farrago, one of the main characters, a keen, practical man, with an abounding sense of humor, finds continued amusement in his red-headed Irish servant, Teague O'Regan, who is constantly getting into a stew because of his popularity with the masses. Just here is the main purpose of the book: to show the follies of a young democracy, to illustrate the fact that an unsettled, raw race is not always ready for the duties and responsibilities of the self-government thus suddenly cast upon them. What a politician Teague might have made! He could have had any office from hog-reeve to a seat in Congress, simply because he was " popular with the common people." He was so ignorant that he could not justly hold any position; but what did that matter so long as the free voter liked him? But, alas, how fickle are the free voters!

Appointed collector of the excise in the Alleghanies, he is seized by these same " free people," " the masses," " the voters," tarred and feathered, and borne away to oblivion. My dear, deluded politician, all the people can fool you part of the time; part of the people can fool you all the time; but don't let all the people fool you all the time!

If it had not been for the restraining presence of Captain Farrago, Teague would have been the people's fool for ever and a day. That Farrago himself was possessed of plenty of sense and a shrewd wit may be inferred from his reply to a challenge for a duel. It is a clever bit of ridicule of the " gentlemanly " custom of " defending one's honor."

" ' Sir:

" ' I have two objections to this duel matter. The one is, lest I should hurt you; and the other is, lest you should hurt me. I do not see any good it would do me to put a bullet thro' any part of your body. I could make no use of you when dead for any culinary purpose, as I would a rabbit or turkey. I am no cannibal to feed on the flesh of men. Why then shoot down a human creature, of which I could make no use? A buffalo would be better meat. For though your flesh may be delicate and tender; yet it wants

280

that firmness and consistency which takes and retains salt. At any rate, it would not be fit for long sea voyages. You might make a good barbecue, it is true, being of the nature of a raccoon or an opossum; but people are not in the habit of barbecuing anything human now. As to your hide, it is not worth taking off, being little better than that of a year old colt.

" ' It would seem to me a strange thing to shoot at a man that would stand still to be shot at; inasmuch as I have been heretofore used to shoot at things flying or running or jumping. Were you on a tree now, like a squirrel, endeavoring to hide yourself in the branches, or, like a raccoon, that after much eyeing and spying, I observe at length in the crotch of a tall oak, with bough and leaves intervening, so that I could just get sight of his hinder parts, I should think it pleasurable enough to take a shot at you. But as it is there is no skill or judgment requisite either to discover or take you down.

" ' As to myself, I do not much like to stand in the way of anything harmful. I am under apprehensions you might hit me. That being the case, I think it most advisable to stay at a distance. If you want to try your pistols, take some object, a tree or a barn door about my dimensions. If you hit that, send me word, and I shall acknowledge that if I had been in the same place, you might also have hit me.' "

Teague O'Regan, however, was not possessed of such a supply of common-sense. He was al-

ways at the service of his countrymen. One
day he and the Captain, coming upon an assem-
blage, found the people voting for a legislator.
There were two candidates, the one a man of
considerable intelligence, the other a weaver
who knew almost nothing beyond the trade of
spinning. The people wanted the weaver; he
was popular with the voting classes. Captain
Farrago made a speech against the laborer, and
in the course of his remarks said:

" ' To come from counting threads and adjusting
them to the splits of a reed, to regulate the finances
of a government, would be preposterous; there being
no congruity in the case. There is no analogy between knotting threads and framing laws. . . . Not
that a manufacturer of linen or woolen or other
stuffs, is an inferior character, but a different one
from that which ought to be employed in affairs of
state. . . . When you go to the senate house, the ap-
plication to you will not be to warp a web; but to
make laws for the commonwealth. Now, suppose that
the making of these laws requires a knowledge of
commerce or of the interests of agriculture, or those
principles upon which the different manufactures de-
pend, what service could you render? . . . It is a
disagreeable thing for a man to be laughed at, and
there is no way of keeping one's self from it but by
avoiding all affectation.' "

But even while this was going on, the people took a sudden liking for red-headed O'Regan, while he on his part was just as suddenly seized with a liking for the legislature. Naturally the Captain seriously objected; the people, however, " were tenacious of their choice, and insisted on giving Teague their suffrages; and by the frown upon their brows, seemed to indicate resentment at what had been said, as directly charging them with want of judgment. . . . 'It is a very strange thing,' said one of them, . . . 'that after having conquered Burgoyne and Cornwallis, and got a government of our own, we cannot put in it whom we please. . . . He may not be yet skilled in the matter, but there is a good day coming. We will empower him; and it is better to trust a plain man like him than one of your high-flyers that will make laws to suit their own purposes.' "

As a last resort, Farrago took Teague aside and showed him the evils of the statesman's life. " 'When a man becomes a member of a public body, he is like a raccoon or other beast that climbs up the fork of a tree; the boys pushing at him with pitchforks or throwing stones or shooting at him with an arrow, the dogs barking in the mean time. One will find fault with your not speaking; another with your speaking, if you speak at all. They will put you in the newspapers and ridicule you as a perfect beast. There is what they call the caricatura, that is, representing you with a dog's head or a cat's claw. As you have a red head they will very probably make a fox of you, or a sorrel horse, or a brindled cow. It is the devil in hell to be exposed to the squibs and crackers of the gazette wits and publications.' " Teague decided to decline the honor with thanks.

We all know how a raw, uncultured community likes to show off what little learning it does possess. Just so it must have been in the early days of our Republic. A Philosophical Society had been formed, declares the author, and Teague—think of it!—had been invited to become a member! " It was necessary . . . for the candidates to procure some token of a philosophic turn of mind, such as the skin of a dead cat, or some odd kind of a mouse-trap; or have phrases in their mouths about minerals and petrifactions; so as to support some idea of natural knowledge, and pass muster. There was one who got in, by finding accidentally the tail of a rabbit, which had been taken off in a boy's trap. . . . The beard of an old fox, taken off and dried in the sun, was the means of introducing one whom I knew very well. . . . It happened as the Captain was riding this day, and Teague trotting after him, he saw a large owl that had been shot by somebody, and was placed in the crotch of a tree. . . . The Captain being struck with it, as somewhat larger than such birds usually are, desired Teague to reach it to him; and tying it to the hinder part of his saddle, rode along." As they came into the village, members of the Society saw the bird, marvelled at it, and at once proposed to elect Teague to membership.

Of course, Farrago felt duty-bound to offer some objections. You may have noticed that there are always some hard-headed fellows who oppose "the will of the people." Farrago's objections were all in vain. " Said the philosopher, at the first institution of the society, by Dr. Franklin and others, it was put upon a narrow basis, and only men of science were considered proper to compose it; and this might be a necessary policy at that time. . . . The matter stands now on a broad and catholic bottom; and like the gospel itself, it is our orders, 'to go out into the highways and hedges, and compel them to come in.' There are hundreds whose names you may see on our list, who are not more instructed than this lad of yours.''

As in many another emergency, the Captain's last and only successful appeal was to Teague's cowardice. He described the hardships liable to come to a member of the learned Philosophical Society, and then stressed the dangers of it all. '' 'It is their great study to find curiosities; and because this man saw you coming after me, with a red head, trotting like an Esquimaux Indian, it has struck his mind to pick you up and pass you for one. Nay, it is possible they may intend worse; and when they have examined you awhile, take the skin off you, and pass you for an overgrown otter, or a musk-rat, or some outlandish animal, for which they will themselves invent a name.' '' Again the Irishman declined the honor.

Do you not see that it is all a protest against too much liberty to an unprepared people, an argument against the infallibility of democracy? In its day the book was really needed; for there seemed to be imminent danger of our nation's becoming freedom-mad and filling the halls of congress with the butcher, the baker, and the candlestick maker, instead of with oil-magnates, coal-barons, and railroad manipulators. And, luckily, the lesson was taught where it was most needed; for, as we have seen, the book had its greatest popularity in the primitive society of the new West.

How closely American humor of those days clings to the history of the nation! First it portrays the humor of founding a new civilization; it passes to a satirical expression of the people's discontent; it aids with its sarcasm in a deadly struggle against tyranny; and now it turns and warns its people of their extravagance in a new-found liberty. Perhaps nothing has been more important in influencing the development of America's political history than the humor of the American press.

In these later colonial times everybody laughed. We gain such mistaken ideas from our books of history concerning the sombreness and solemnity of the old days. Every statesman, nearly every preacher, unbent now and then, in private at least, and indulged in wit. John Adams wrote some very passable humor; Jefferson is credited with numerous brilliant passes; pious Timothy Dwight, as we have seen, loved to crack a joke on his theological foes; and Governor William Livingston, of New Jersey, known as "the Don Quixote of the Jerseys," wrote so many laughable squibs that at last the people of his State protested, and passed resolutions declaring it indecorous in their Chief Magistrate to be so funny. Even grave George Washington now and then attempted humor. Does he not approach it in this letter describing a soldier's dinner?

"Since our arrival at this happy spot, we have had a ham, sometimes a shoulder of bacon, to grace the head of the table; a piece of roast beef adorns the foot; and a dish of beans or greens, almost imperceptible, decorates the centre. When the cook has a mind to cut a figure, which I presume will be the case tomorrow, we have two beef-steak pies, or dishes of crabs, in addition, one on each side of the centre dish, dividing the space and reducing the distance between dish and dish to about six feet, which without them would be near twelve feet apart. Of late he has had the surprising sagacity to discover that apples will make pies; and it is a question, if, in the violence of his efforts, we do not get one of apples instead of having both of beef-steaks. If the ladies can put up with such entertainment, and will submit to partake of it on plates, once tin but now iron (not become so by the labor of scouring), I shall be happy to see them. . . ."

I

No study of colonial humor would be complete without some mention of the dramatic wit of the period. Notwithstanding the current opinion to the contrary, many of our ancestors of New England and New York and Pennsylvania went to plays and enjoyed them. Would that this were the place to enter into some discussion of the early American theatre; it is a genuinely interesting subject. We have seen that performances were given in Williamsburg, Virginia, and Charleston, South Carolina, as early as 1716, and in houses built for such a purpose; while dramatic performances were not rare in New York and Philadelphia as far back as 1760. In 1792 plays were presented in Boston under the name of " dramatic recitation," so as not to conflict with the laws on " stage plays." The bill was repealed in 1793, and that same year the Federal Street Theatre was built, and on February 4, 1794, was opened for public acting.

The first play written in America for actual presentation seems to have been Thomas Godfrey's *Prince of Parthia,* composed in 1758 and offered in 1759 to the once famous American Company at Philadelphia. It was a dignified, stiff piece of work; but it might have succeeded with the uncritical colonists of that day. For some unknown reason, however, it was never produced. As early as 1766 a play based on an American theme, *Ponteach, or, The Savages of America,* had been written by Major Robert Rogers, an officer in the French and Indian War; but we have no record of its performance. Perhaps it was best that it was born to blush unseen; for it had some cause to blush. It was thoroughly conventional; every Indian in it was a cultured gentleman. We know, too, that in 1767 there was published in New York City an amusing satirical play called *Disenchantment, or, The Force of Credulity, a New American Comic Opera of Three Acts,* written by one " Andrew Barton." But it was so effective in its personal allusions that it was withdrawn after its first rehearsal at Philadelphia. Verily, American drama was having a hard struggle to be born.

290

In 1774 dramatic literature came to its own as a political agency. In that year we find Jonathan Sewall, hot-headed old Tory of Massachusetts, writing a crude but nevertheless effective colloquy entitled, *The Americans Roused, in a Cure for the Spleen, or, Amusement for a Winter's Evening: Being the Substance of a Conversation on the Times over a Friendly Tankard and Pipe.* What a fine appearance all that would have made on ye old time bill-board! Again, however, the piece was not publicly presented; but, as it was widely read and as it ridiculed the work of the first Continental Congress, it did indeed arouse the Americans. About the same time Madam Mercy Warren, " the historical, philosophical, poetical, and satirical consort of . . . General James Warren of Plymouth "—so the quaint announcement put it—wrote two plays dealing with the political situation of the period. One of these was *The Adulator: a Tragedy, as it is now Acted in Upper Servia.* Of course, "Upper Servia" was nothing more nor less than Boston, while Brutus, Cassius, Marcus, and the other classic characters were our more modern friends, John Adams, Samuel Adams,

Hancock, and so on. If any Englishman ever read that dramatic sketch, he must have been decidedly ashamed of himself; for Mercy Warren portrayed the whole British race as a multitude of devils. Her other play, *The Group,* was published in 1775. Various indignant Royalists of New England found themselves presented to the public under the astonishing names of Beau Trumps, Scriblerius Fribble, Simple Sapling, Sir Sparrow Spendall, Brigadier Hateall, and Judge Meagre. Perhaps a part of one of the Judge's speeches will give an idea of the general flavor:

" I hate the people who, no longer gulled,
  See through the schemes of our aspiring clan.
  And from the rancor of my venomed mind,
  I look askance on all the human race;
  And if they're not to be appalled by fear,
  I wish the earth might drink that vital stream
  That warms the heart and feeds the manly glow—
  The love inherent, planted in the breast,
  To equal liberty conferred on man
  By Him who formed the peasant and the King."

The next year, 1776, there was published a play not quite so long as its title would indicate—*The Fall of British Tyranny: or Ameri-*

can Liberty Triumphant. The First Campaign. A Tragi-Comedy of Five Acts, as Lately Planned at the Royal Theatrum Pandemonium at St. James. The drama is really a portrayal of all the important events in the Revolution up to the date when the play appeared, and the plot, as daring in location as in time, hops from one continent to another with an agility equalled only by the author's contempt for the classic rules of play-writing. Perhaps we can realize something of its rough humor from this bit of a scene. The British generals and a British admiral are holding a council of war. They cannot see what to do with these stubborn American rustics. The Battle of Bunker Hill is just over, and Lord Boston is complaining of the way these colonists fight. A loud squabbling results; but the admiral breaks in upon it in true sailor fashion:

" Damn it, don't let us kick up a dust among ourselves, to be laughed at fore and aft. This is a hell of a council of war,—though I believe it will turn out one before we're done.

.   .   .   .

Lord Boston: Well, gentlemen, what are we met here for?

Admiral Tombstone: Who the devil should know if you don't? Damn it, didn't you send for us?

.   .   .   .

Clinton: The provincials are vastly strong, and seem no novices in the art of war. 'Tis true, we gained the hill at last, but of what advantage is it to us? None. The loss of fourteen hundred as brave men as Britain can boast of is a melancholy consideration, and must make our most sanguinary friends in England abate of their vigor.

Elbow Room: I never saw or read of any battle equal to it. . . . No laurels there!

Mr. Caper: No, nor triumphs neither. I regret in particular the number of brave officers that fell that day, many of whom were of the first families in England.

Admiral Tombstone: Aye, a damned affair, indeed! Many powdered beaux—petit maitres—fops—fribbles —skip jackets—macaronies—jack puddings—noblemen's bastards and whores' sons fell that day; and my poor marines stood no more chance with 'em than a cat in hell without claws.

Lord Boston: It can't be helped, Admiral. What is to be done next?

Admiral Tombstone: Done?—why, what the devil have you done? Nothing yet, but eat Paramount's beef, and steal a few Yankee sheep; and that, it seems, is now become a damned lousy, beggarly trade, too; for you haven't left yourselves a mouthful to eat.''

Late in the winter of 1775 General Burgoyne wrote for the amusement of his officers and the Tories a farce called *The Blockade,*—a play which the aforesaid officers presented with great gusto in Faneuil Hall, Boston. But the sad day for the evacuation came in March, 1776, and then it was that some American, probably Mercy Warren, wrote a farce on the farce, and gave it the happy title of *The Block-Heads, or the Affrighted Officers.* It afforded many a laugh to the patriots, for it dealt with the surprise felt by the British when they awoke one morning to find Washington and his ragamuffins encamped upon the hills about Boston. Thus the merry war of words continued. Dramatic humor, in short, served the country in just the same way and with just as much zeal as did the newspapers and the magazines and the innumerable pamphlets of the day.

ROYALL TYLER

Few if any of these early attempts deserve the name of dramas; some were never acted; some were never intended for acting; they sometimes had simply the dramatic feature of dialogue or conversation. The first American

comedy regularly produced was *The Contrast,
a Comedy in Five Acts: written by a Citizen of
the United States,* played at the John Street
Theatre in New York in 1787. The " citizen
of the United States," it was soon known, was
Royall Tyler (1757-1826). It would not do to
attempt to rehearse with any detail the deeds
of Tyler's life; it would require another volume. He felt capable to undertake any task,
no matter how novel or difficult. We have
heard that " fools rush in where angels fear to
tread;" but this Tyler was no fool. He became a famous jurist in his day; he was aide-
de-camp to General Benjamin Lincoln when
that soldier undertook to squelch Shay's Rebellion; and he wrote informing magazine articles on all sorts of subjects. He went abroad,
and the result was his entertaining *Yankee in
London* (1809). His contributions to the
Farmer's Weekly Museum (Walpole, N. H.)
were widely copied and made his name known
in every New England home. His *Reports of
Cases in the Supreme Court of Vermont*
(1809) showed him to be an attorney of much
acumen. He was forever busy—a rather relia-
ble sign of genius, by the way.

While in New York, seeing about affairs connected with Shay's Rebellion, he concluded that
he could write a play, and *The Contrast* proved
it. It was acted by that famous " American
Company " in April, 1787, and was such a success that Tyler felt encouraged to try his hand
again. The next month he produced *May Day
in Town, or New York in an Uproar,* a comic
opera in two acts. Ten years later, in 1797,
his *Good Spec, or Land in the Moon,* caught
the public fancy in Boston. Royall Tyler
might have made a famous playwright, if he
had not been such a successful judge.

Strange to say, this first attempt, *The Contrast,* is not nearly so egotistical as most first
attempts in literature are. In the " advertisement " the author puts forward the following
excuse: " In justice to the Author it may be
proper to observe that this Comedy has many
claims to the public indulgence, independent of
its intrinsic merits: It is the first essay of
American genius in a difficult species of compo-
sition; it was written by one who never criti-
cally studied the rules of the drama, and, indeed,
has seen but few of the exhibitions of the stage;
it was undertaken and finished in the course of

three weeks; and the profits of one night's performance were appropriated to the benefit of the sufferers by the fire of Boston.''

And what is our first regularly acted comedy about? Well, it would show once more, if you please, the difference between the '' good old times '' and these degenerate modern days. But let a few lines from the Prologue tell you about it:

'' Exult each patriot heart!—this night is shown
    A piece which we may fairly call our own;
    Where the proud titles of ' My Lord! Your Grace! '
    To humble ' Mr.' and plain ' Sir ' give place.
    Our author pictures not from foreign climes
    The fashions or the follies of the times;
    But has confined the subject of his work
    To the gay scenes—the circles of New York.''

The purpose being stated, Tyler proceeds to illustrate it. The first scene of the first act will give an idea of how the '' contrast '' will be presented; for here at the very beginning the idle chat of the '' weaker sex '' portrays the shameful depravity of our modern times. What a blessing that we can so easily shift the burden of our wickedness upon *woman!* Adam, the first man, did it,—but let us turn to our comedy. Charlotte and Letitia, two colonial damsels, are talking.

"*Letitia:* And so, Charlotte, you really think the pocket-hoop unbecoming.

Charlotte: No, I don't say so. It may be very becoming to saunter round the house of a rainy day; to visit my grandmamma, or to go to Quakers' meeting; but to swim in a minuet, with the eyes of fifty well-dressed beaux upon me, to trip it in the Mall, or walk on the Battery, give me the luxurious, jaunty, flowing bell-hoop. It would have delighted you to have seen me the last evening, my charming girl! I was dangling o'er the Battery with Billy Dimple; a knot of young fellows were upon the platform; as I passed them I faltered with one of the most bewitching false steps you ever saw, and then recovered myself with such a pretty confusion, flirting my hoop to discover a jet-black shoe and brilliant buckle. Gad! how my little heart thrilled to hear the confused raptures of— 'Demme, Jack, what a delicate foot!' 'Ha! General, what a well turned——'

Let.: Fie! fie! Charlotte (*stopping her mouth*). I protest you are quite a libertine.

Charl.: Why, my dear little prude, are we not all such libertines? Do you think when I sat tortured two hours under the hands of my friseur, and an hour more at my toilet, that I had any thoughts of my aunt Susan or my cousin Betsey? though they are both allowed to be critical judges of dress.

Let.: Why, who should we dress to please, but those who are judges of its merit?

Charl.: Why, a creature who does not know *Buffon* from *Souflee*—Man!—my Letitia—Man! for whom we dress, walk, dance, talk, lisp, languish, and smile. . . . Why, I 'll undertake with one flirt of this hoop to bring more beaux to my feet in one week than the grave Maria and her sentimental circle can do by sighing sentiment till their hairs are gray.

. . . .

Let.: It is whispered that if Maria gives her hand to Mr. Dimple it will be without her heart.

Charl.: Though the giving of the heart is one of the last of all laughable considerations in the marriage of a girl of spirit, yet I should like to hear what anti-quated notions the dear little piece of old fashioned prudery has got in her head.

. . . .

Let.: . . . Why, she read Sir Charles Grandison, Clarissa Harlow, Shenstone, and the Sentimental Journey, and between whiles, as I said, Billy's letters. But as her taste improved, her love declined. The contrast was so striking betwixt the good-sense of her books and the flimsiness of her love-letters, that she discovered she had unthinkingly engaged her hand without her heart; and then the whole transaction managed by the old folks now appeared so unsentimental and looked so like bargaining for a bale of goods that she found she ought to have rejected, according to every rule of romance, even the man of her choice if imposed upon her in that manner. Clary Harlow would have scorned such a match.

Charl.: Well, how was it on Mr. Dimple's return? Did he meet a more favorable reception than his letters?

Let.: Much the same. She spoke of him with respect abroad and with contempt in her closet. She watched his conduct and conversation, and found that he had by travelling acquired the wickedness of Lovelace without his wit, and the politeness of Sir Charles Grandison without his generosity. The ruddy youth who washed his face at the cistern every morning, and swore and looked eternal love and constancy, was now metamorphosed into a flippant, pallid, polite beau, who devotes the morning to his toilet, reads a few pages of Chesterfield's letters, and then minces out, to put the infamous principles in practice upon every woman he meets.''

Thus the conversation proceeds, relating the idle nothings of the day. And thus, too, our New England lawyer-dramatist strove to arouse once more the waning patriotism of the metropolis of the New World, and, in a new field, to make American humor a useful agency to American democracy. The Revolution over, however, and the nation on the highway to prosperity, most of the plays ceased to deal with the

dangers of the day, and existed merely for the
pleasure that they gave. Some of them were
crude; some of them were rude; and several
of them were vulgar to an extent that aston-
ishes us of scarcely a century later. All of them
were lively and hearty, however, while not a
few contained many a good laugh and many a
jingle that caught the public ear. Now and
then one of these old lyrics is wafted down to
our day; such as, the Sleighing Song from the
once popular *Better Sort, or the Girl of Spirit*
(1789). Hear a few lines from a "popular
song " of colonial days:

> " What pleasure can compare
> To a sleighing with the fair
> In the evening, the evening, in cold and frosty
> weather?
> When rapidly we go
> As we jingle o'er the snow,
> And tantarra, huzza! And tantarra, huzza!
> And tantarra! sings every brave fellow!

> " When to Watertown we get,
> And the turkey's on the spit,
> And we dance, boys, and dance, boys, and drive away
> all sorrow,
> 'Tis then your milk and tea
> Give place to strong sangree,

And we banish, huzza! We banish, huzza!
And we banish the cares of to-morrow!

     •   •   •   •   •

" Now for Boston we prepare,
And the night is cold and clear,
And we're stowing close, we're stowing close, because
    it's chilly weather.
O then what fun we feel
When the sleigh it takes a heel,
And we're huddled, huzza! And we're huddled,
    huzza!
And we're huddled, brave boys, altogether!

" 'Tis then the ladies cry,
O lud!—O dear!—O my!
And we scrabble, boys, we scrabble, boys, all from the
    snowy weather.
Then in the sleigh again
Do we scamper o'er the plain,
And tantarra, huzza, tantarra, huzza!
And tantarra! sings every brave fellow! "

WILLIAM DUNLAP

As one looks over these first attempts in American drama one is inclined to wonder why our nation has reached no greater heights in this field of literature. There was life in those old plays; there was frequently a vigorous bit of rhetoric; there was undoubtedly wit. We might point out as another example, the first American tragedy regularly produced, *Leicester,* performed at the old John Street Theatre in New York in 1794,—a play so high in tone and striking in situation that it is by no means to be sneered at. Its author, William Dunlap (1766-1839), wrote at the age of twenty-three a successful comedy entitled *The Father of an Only Child;* and one may well doubt whether there is living to-day in America a man of twenty-three who could equal it. The fame of this William Dunlap has not passed away even in this day. The Dunlap Society of New York City, in its efforts to encourage American art, has done his name honor. For he was an artist as well as a dramatist; his series of pictures on Scriptural subjects, once exhibited throughout America, do indeed great credit to an art in its infancy. As the founder of the National Academy of Design, and author of the *History of the Rise and Progress of the Art of Design in the United States* (1834), he showed his sincere zeal for one of his professions; while through his *History of the American Theatre* (1832) and his pleasing plays, he showed his knowledge and talent in the other.

That the old days were not destitute of humor I hope I have proved. Extracts from Dunlap's *Father of an Only Child* would but add to the proof. See how natural the dialogue is in this old-time drama. Mr. and Mrs. Racket are seated at breakfast. Mr. Racket has doubtless been out late the night before, as he now has a suspicious black patch on his nose. With his weak and sleepy eyes, he is trying at one and the same time to read a paper and listen to his wife's morning discourse. I leave it to my married readers as to whether there is any truth in the description.

"*Racket.* Yaw! yaw! Curse me if I can see distinctly this morning. Is it that I lack sleep, or do the printers lack new types? Go on, my dear, go on: I believe you were speaking. (*Reads again.*)

Mrs. Rack. (*Rising and speaking aside.*) This provoking indifference is not to be borne! I must rouse him from it, or lose all hopes of happiness. (*To him.*) Let me tell you, Mr. Racket, your present behavior is neither manly nor polite. Contrary to the advice of Colonel Campbell, my guardian, I threw myself and my fortune into your arms, blindly excusing, as the levities of youth, your noted propensities to vicious dissipation.

Rack. (*Reads.*) 'A majority of thirty-one in favor of adopting it with amendments.' Pray sit down, my dear; you will fatigue yourself; pray sit down.

Mrs. Rack. Sir, this is adding insult to injury! In marrying you, I risked the displeasure of all my friends: and though the excellent Colonel Campbell, my second father, yielded to my will, I hazarded by my conduct that paternal love which was the first joy of my heart. On your faith I staked all.

Rack. Let me tell you, my life, you are a desperate gambler! After such a confession, can you ever have the face to find fault with my staking a few hundreds on a card?

Mrs. Rack. I deserve the reproach, sir; and if the game was yet to play—— (*Pauses.*)

Rack. Come, there is some spirit in that. Go on, madam.

Mrs. Rack. Perhaps——

Rack. You would play the same stake again.

Mrs. Rack. What is my gain?

Rack. A husband.

Mrs. Rack. Whose face I never see, except when excess and riot have made it unfit for public view.

Rack. (*Reads.*) ' And we hope our virtuous example will be followed by all our fellow citizens.'

Mrs. Rack. (*Walking in agitation.*) Virtuous example truly! O, Mr. Racket, we have been married but one year, and——

Rack. (*Rising and yawning.*) No more! It has been a curst long year! ''

II

It is high time that we bring our discussion of colonial humor to a close. How much it is necessary to omit! We have but noted here and there the more conspicuous flows in the never-ceasing current of laughter. From 1607 until the days when the Republic had taken a permanent place among nations, America was never without its store of witty intellects. True, there were blue laws, witch burnings, and Indian massacres; but in spite of these and the sorrows, superstitions, and unbending theologies the people saw much of the sunshine and the gladness of this world. Often indeed their laughter was full of bitter, Hebraic taunting; but there were bitter tyrants and bitter hardships, be it remembered, and it was something of a wonder that at times there was any joy whatever. It is a remarkable testimony to the sturdiness of the American people, that, in spite of the terrors of the wilderness and the terrors of tyrannical misrule, they have retained the happy faculty of being able to see a joke and return it with interest. May they never lose that faculty; for as an old colonist, Jonathan Sewall of New Hampshire, declares in his *Eulogy on Laughing,*

"It makes the wheels of nature gliblier play;
   Dull care suppresses; smoothes life's thorny way;
   Propels the dancing current thro' each vein;
   Braces the nerves; corroborates the brain;
   Shakes every muscle, and throws off the spleen."

BIBLIOGRAPHY

The following books and periodicals will be found most useful in the study of early humor in America. A number of these publications may be secured in any good public or college library; many of them, unfortunately, are to be found in only the largest and oldest collections. It will be a glad day for students of American literature when some society or patriotic individual can furnish the financial means for the publication in inexpensive form of these interesting and valuable colonial writings.

ADAMS, JOHN: *Letters*, Boston, 1841.
ALLEN: *American Biographical Dictionary*, Boston, 1857.
ALLIBONE: *Dictionary of Authors*, New York.
ALSOP: *Political Green House*, Hartford, 1799.
American Antiquarian Society Proceedings.
American Chronicles of the Times, Philadelphia, 1774–75.
American Museum, Philadelphia, 1787–92.
ANDRE: *The Cow-Chace*, New York, 1780.
ARBUTHNOT: *History of John Bull*, New York, 1789.
Aristocracy, Philadelphia, 1795.
Atlantic Monthly, Boston.
BANCROFT: *History of the United States*, New York, 1791.
BARLOW: *Columbiad*, Philadelphia, 1807.
BARLOW: *Conspiracy of Kings*, London, 1792.
BARLOW: *Vision of Columbus*, Hartford, 1787.
BARTON: *Disappointment*, New York, 1767.

BIBLIOGRAPHY

Battle of Brooklyn: A Farce, New York, 1776.

BEERS: *A Century of American Literature,* New York, 1878.

BEERS: *Initial Studies in American Letters,* New York, 1892.

BIGELOW: *Life of Benjamin Franklin,* New York.

BLAUVELT: *Fashion's Analysis,* New York, 1807.

Blockheads, The, A Farce, Boston, 1776.

BRACKENRIDGE: *Battle of Bunker Hill,* Philadelphia, 1776.

BRACKENRIDGE: *Death of General Montgomery,* Philadelphia, 1777.

BRACKENRIDGE: *Modern Chivalry,* Pittsburgh, 1804.

BRACKENRIDGE: *Six Political Discourses,* Lancaster, 1778.

BRADSHAW: *Southern Poetry Prior to 1860,* Richmond, Virginia, 1900.

BURTON: *Cyclopedia of Wit and Humor,* New York, 1858.

BYLES: *Poems on Several Occasions,* Boston, 1744.

BYLES: *The Comet,* Boston, 1744.

CAMPBELL: *Anne Bradstreet,* Boston, 1891.

CAREY: *The Plagi-Scurriliad,* Philadelphia, 1786.

CAREY: *The Porcupiniad,* Philadelphia, 1799.

CLEMENS (TWAIN): *Library of American Humor,* New York.

Columbian Muse, New York, 1794.

Connecticut Journal and New Haven Post-Boy, 1770–73.

COOK: *Sot-Weed Factor,* Maryland Historical Society Fund Publications, 1900, No. 36.

COOK: *Sot-Weed Redivivus,* Maryland Historical Society Fund Publications, 1900, No. 36.

DELANCEY: *Philip Freneau,* 1891.

DELAPLAINE: *Repository of Lives and Portraits of Distinguished American Characters,* Philadelphia, 1815–18.

Dictionary of National Biography, London, 1890.

BIBLIOGRAPHY

DRAKE: *Dictionary of American Biography*, Boston, 1872.

DUTTON: *Present State of Literature*, Hartford, 1800.

DUYCKINCK: *Cyclopedia of American Literature*, New York, 1875.

DUYCKINCK: *Poems by Philip Freneau*, Philadelphia.

DWIGHT: *Triumph of Infidelity*, 1788.

Echo, The, Hartford, 1807.

ELIOT: *Biographical Dictionary*, Boston, 1809.

Encyclopædia Britannica.

EVANS: *American Bibliography*, Chicago, 1903–05.

EVERETT: *Poets of Connecticut*, Hartford, 1844.

Fall of British Tyranny; A Tragi-Comedy, Philadelphia, 1776.

FESSENDEN: *Democracy Unveiled*, Boston, 1805.

FESSENDEN: *Original Poems*, London, 1804.

FESSENDEN: *Terrible Tractoratum*, New York, 1804.

FISHER: *Men, Women and Manners of Colonial Times*, Philadelphia, 1898.

FISKE: *Appleton's Cyclopædia of American Biography*, New York, 1889.

FORD: *Beginnings of American Dramatic Literature*, New York.

FRENEAU: *Poems Written and Published during the American Revolution*, Philadelphia, 1809.

FRENEAU: *Miscellaneous Works*, Philadelphia, 1788.

GOODRICH: *Recollections of a Life Time*, New York, 1857.

GREEN: *Entertainment for a Winter's Evening*, Boston, 1750.

GREGOIRE: *Critical Observations on the Columbiad*, Washington, 1809.

GRIEVOUS, PETER: *Congratulatory Epistle to the Redoubtable Peter Porcupine*, Philadelphia, 1796.

GRISWOLD: *Curiosities of American Literature*, New York.

GRISWOLD: *Female Poets of America*, New York, 1848.

GRISWOLD: *Poets and Poetry of America*, Philadelphia, 1843.

HAVEN: *Catalogue of American Publications*, Albany, 1874.

HART: *Manual of American Literature*, New York.

HOLLIDAY: *A History of Southern Literature*, New York, 1906.

HOLLIDAY: *The Literature of Colonial Virginia*, New York, 1907.

HOLLIDAY: *Three Centuries of Southern Poetry*, Nashville, 1908.

HOPKINS, LEMUEL: *The Guillotine*, Philadelphia, 1796.

HOPKINS, LEMUEL: *The Democratiad*, Philadelphia, 1795.

HOPKINS, JOSEPH: *The Hamiltoniad*, Philadelphia, 1804.

HOPKINSON: *Miscellaneous Essays and Occasional Writings*, New York, 1804.

HOPKINSON: *The Old Farm and the New Farm*, New York, 1864.

HOWELL: *A Fan for Fanning*, North Carolina Magazine, February, 1859.

HOWS: *American Poems*, New York.

HOWS: *Golden Leaves from American Poets*, New York.

HOWS: *Poetry of the People*, New York.

HUMPHREYS: *Miscellaneous Works*, New York, 1804.

JACKSON: *Literary History of Colonial Pennsylvania*, Lancaster, 1906.

KETTELL: *Specimens of American Poetry*, Boston, 1829.

KNAPP: *Eminent Lawyers, Statesmen, and Men of Letters*, Boston, 1821.

LIVINGSTON: *Democracy*, New York, 1790.

LOSSING: Trumbull's *McFingal*, New York, 1881.

Loyalist Poetry of the Revolution, Philadelphia, 1857.

Massachusetts Historical Society Proceedings.

MCMASTERS: *Benjamin Franklin as a Man of Letters*, Boston, 1895.

MITCHELL: *American Lands and Letters*, New York, 1897.

MOORE: *Diary of the American Revolution*, New York, 1860.

MOORE: *Illustrated Ballad History of the American Revolution*, New York, 1876.

MOORE: *Songs and Ballads of the American Revolution*, New York, 1856.

MORRIS: *Half-Hours with the Best Humorous Authors*, Philadelphia.

MORSE: *Benjamin Franklin*, Boston, 1889.

Motley Assembly, The, A Farce, Boston, 1779.

MUNFORD: *Poems*, Richmond, 1798.

National Portrait Gallery of Distinguished Americans, Philadelphia, 1835.

NICHOLS: *Select Collection of Poems*, 1780.

ODELL: *The American Times*, New York, 1780.

Olio, Philadelphia, 1801.

ONDERDONK: *History of American Verse*, Chicago, 1901.

OSGOOD: *American Colonies in the Seventeenth Century*, New York, 1904.

OTIS: *American Verse*, New York, 1909.

PATTEE: *Poems of Philip Freneau,* Princeton, 1902–07.

Pennsylvania Historical Society Publications.

Pennsylvania Magazine of History and Biography.

Philadelphiensis, Philadelphia, 1762.

"Pilgarlic": The Albaniad, 1791.

Prince Society Publications, Boston.

Rhode Island Historical Society Publications.

RICHARDSON: *American Literature*, New York, 1887–89.

RIGGS: *The Anarchiad*, New Haven, 1861.

RUTHERFORD: *American Literature*, Atlanta.

BIBLIOGRAPHY

SABIN: *Bibliotheca Americana,* New York, 1868.

SABINE: *Biographical Sketches of Loyalists,* Boston, 1864.

SANDERSON: *Biography of the Signers of the Declaration,* Philadelphia, 1827.

SARGENT: *Loyalist Poetry of the Revolution,* Philadelphia, 1857.

SARGENT: *Loyal Verses of Stansbury and Odell,* Albany, 1860.

SEARS: *American Literature in the Colonial and National Periods,* Boston, 1902.

SEARSON: *Poems on Various Subjects,* Philadelphia, 1797.

SEDGWICK: *William Livingston,* New York, 1833.

SEWALL: *Miscellaneous Poems,* Portsmouth, 1801.

SEWALL: *The American Roused,* Reprinted by James Harrington, New York.

Sewanee Review, Sewanee, Tennessee.

SHEA: *Alsop's Character of the Province of Maryland,* New York, 1869.

SHEA: *Early Southern Tracts,* 1866.

SMITH: *American Poems,* 1793.

SMITH: *Foundation of the American Colonies.*

South Atlantic Quarterly, Durham, North Carolina.

SPARKS: *Library of American Biography,* Boston, 1847.

SPRAGUE: *Annals of the American Pulpit,* New York, 1869.

Spunkiad, The, Newburgh, 1798.

STEDMAN: *American Anthology,* Boston.

STEDMAN: *Poets of America,* Boston, 1885.

STEDMAN and HUTCHINSON: *Library of American Literature,* New York, 1889.

STONE: *Ballads and Poems Relating to the Burgoyne Campaign,* Albany, 1893.

TAPPAN: *America's Literature,* Boston.

THOMAS: *History of Printing in America.*

BIBLIOGRAPHY

THOMPSON: *New England's Crisis,* In the Club of Odd Volumes, Boston, 1894.

TOUCHSTONE: *The House of Wisdom in a Bustle,* Philadelphia, 1798.

TRENT: *History of American Literature,* New York, 1903.

TRENT and WELLS: *Colonial Prose and Poetry,* New York, 1901.

TRUMBULL: *Poetical Works,* Hartford, 1820.

TUDOR: *Life of James Otis.*

TYLER: *History of American Literature during the Colonial Times,* New York.

TYLER: *Literary History of the American Revolution,* New York, 1897.

TYLER: *Three Men of Letters,* New York.

WARREN: *The Adulateur,* Boston, 1775.

WARREN: *The Group,* Boston, 1775.

WARREN: *Poems Dramatic and Miscellaneous,* Boston, 1790.

WATSON: *Annals of Philadelphia,* Philadelphia.

WEGELIN: *Early American Poetry,* New York, 1903.

WENDELL: *Literary History of America,* Boston, 1900.

WHIPPLE: *American Literature,* Boston, 1899.

WILLIAMS: *The Hamiltoniad,* Boston, 1804.

WITHERSPOON, JOHN: *The Works of,* Edinburgh, 1805.

WOODBERRY: *America in Literature,* New York, 1903.

WRIGHT: *Poetry and Poets of Connecticut,* Papers of the New Haven Colony Historical Society.

WYNNE: *Byrd Manuscripts,* 1866.

INDEX

317

INDEX

318

INDEX

319

INDEX